"Part poet, part philosopher, part penite; server and exquisite writer, Suanne Camfield is above all a coach like her father, although this time she encourages us all to a deeper experience of the Stirring and the Becoming. *The Sound of a Million Deams* is a book to read slowly and savor long."

Os Guinness, author of *The Call*

"From the first page, I was drawn into one woman's honest journey through broken dreams and unrealized expectations, into the darkest places of her humanity and out the other side. There she finds herself, finds grace, finds wisdom. This is a beautifully written, introspective, and achingly honest book with so much to discover and savor."

Susy Flory, author and director, West Coast Christian Writers Conference

"In her beautifully written book, Suanne Camfield invites us to uncover our dreams, even those that lie shattered on the ground. By vulnerably sharing her own story, she encourages us to dig deep and interact with our dreams in a way that moves us toward who we really are, not just what we want to do."

Anita Lustrea, media coach, author, and spiritual director

"Few books so brilliantly and beautifully describe the process by which one awakens to a personal dream and then dares to discipline oneself to pursue it as this amazing breakout work by Suanne Camfield. In the course of describing the fears, tears, and laughter that marked her own journey toward fulfillment, Camfield inspires all of us to begin listening for the yearning voice in ourselves that might be calling us to the life we are meant to live."

Daniel Meyer, author of *Discovering God, Witness Essentials*

"Suanne Camfield's writing is vivid and lyrical, nearly every sentence like a pearl plucked from the mouth of an oyster. This book has enriched my life, daring me not just to dream but to become."

Jen Pollock Michel, author of *Teach Us to Want* and *Keeping Place*

"With artful and energetic prose, Suanne Camfield has written an original and honest memoir of her life with all its beauty, complexity, and passion. As you read *The Sound of a Million Dreams* you will find yourself in the company of a woman on a relentless quest to understand and trust the stirring within her to follow a lifelong dream. She will put words to the very experiences you've had in stumbling forward in search of your dreams. And somewhere along the line you will catch her fervor and realize there's no turning back. I commend this book to anyone who loves exquisite writing, rich story, and real life!"

Beth A. Booram, Sustainable Faith Indy, author of *Starting Something New*

"An absolute must-read for anyone who has ever feared, wondered, or second guessed themself as they tried to make their way through this life! Suanne is a master at helping the reader feel known, safe, and befriended on the journey of the soul. She is a brilliant writer and a fellow pilgrim. I giggled and cried and realized again that there are no easy answers. All we have is the sound of our dreams, the vivid echoes and invitations from God to be who we truly are. Find yourself on the journey as you read this book. Camfield is brilliant!"

Tracey Bianchi, worship and teaching pastor, Christ Church of Oak Brook, coauthor of *True You*

"*The Sound of a Million Dreams* simultaneously embraces me right where I am while beautifully beckoning me one step further. Through her intensely honest pilgrimage, Suanne Camfield woos me to become fully who I already am in Jesus."

Elisa Morgan, president emerita, MOPS International, cohost, Discover the Word Radio, author of *The Beauty of Broken*

The Sound of a Million Dreams

AWAKENING TO WHO YOU ARE BECOMING

SUANNE CAMFIELD

FOREWORD BY ADELE AHLBERG CALHOUN

An imprint of InterVarsity Press
Downers Grove, Illinois

InterVarsity Press
P.O. Box 1400, Downers Grove, IL 60515-1426
ivpress.com
email@ivpress.com

InterVarsity Press® is the book-publishing division of InterVarsity Christian Fellowship/USA®, a movement of students and faculty active on campus at hundreds of universities, colleges, and schools of nursing in the United States of America, and a member movement of the International Fellowship of Evangelical Students. For information about local and regional activities, visit intervarsity.org.

All Scripture quotations, unless otherwise indicated, are taken from THE HOLY BIBLE, NEW INTERNATIONAL VERSION®, NIV® Copyright © 1973, 1978, 1984, 2011 by Biblica, Inc.™ Used by permission. All rights reserved worldwide.

While any stories in this book are true, some names and identifying information may have been changed to protect the privacy of individuals.

Cover design: Cindy Kiple
Interior design: Beth McGill
Images: vintage bus: © Mark Owen/Trevillion Images
  butterflies: © proxyminder/iStockphoto

ISBN 978-0-8308-4329-9 (print)
ISBN 978-0-8308-9223-5 (digital)

Printed in the United States of America ∞

Library of Congress Cataloging-in-Publication Data
Names: Camfield, Suanne, 1975- author.
Title: The sound of a million dreams : awakening to who you are becoming /
  Suanne Camfield.
Description: Downers Grove : InterVarsity Press, 2017.
Identifiers: LCCN 2016046964 (print) | LCCN 2016051569 (ebook) (print) |
  LCCN 2016051569 (ebook) | ISBN 9780830843299 (pbk. : alk. paper) | ISBN
  9780830892235 (eBook)
Subjects: LCSH: Dreams—Religious aspects—Christianity. |
  Vocation—Christianity.
Classification: LCC BR115.D74 C36 2017 (print) | LCC BR115.D74 (ebook) | DDC
  248—dc23
LC record available at https://lccn.loc.gov/2016046964

P   21   20   19   18   17   16   15   14   13   12   11   10   9   8   7   6   5   4   3   2   1

Y   34   33   32   31   30   29   28   27   26   25   24   23   22   21   20   19   18   17

For Sadie and Clay

May you always listen to the sound of your dreams,
and have the courage to follow them, wherever God leads.

The future belongs to those who believe in
the beauty of their dreams.

Eleanor Roosevelt

Riches I heed not nor man's empty praise,
Thou my inheritance now and always.

"Be Thou My Vision"

Contents

Foreword

ADELE AHLBERG CALHOUN

There is a Celtic folktale where a host asks his dinner guests, "What is the finest music in the world?" They begin to answer: "The cuckoo in the hedge." "The belling of a stag across the water." "The laughter of a child." "The baying of a wolf pack in the distance." "Lark song at dawn."

It is the bard Fionn that settles the matter: "The music of what happens, that is the finest music in the world."

Suanne Camfield has written the music of what happens.

To read *The Sound of a Million Dreams* is to hear God playing the fine music of memoir through a vulnerable, true voice. In the clamor of a million tasks, Suanne paid attention to what her life was trying to tell her. Pace and busyness don't numb her to "the ache to offer a piece of myself to the world." In the midst of being many things to many people she finds commonplace events—conversations, internships, phone calls, brokenness, friendships, pain, dreams, memories, boredom, longings—can offer a sense of wonder. Which is a wonder!

Sometimes the experiences of life are just points of comparison. You say you traveled to Europe. Your friend compares how many more places they managed to see. Like a knitter rolling yarn into a ball, we can roll strings of experiences into bigger and bigger balls. It's size that counts. But how useful or beautiful or meaningful is a ball of yarn that doesn't get knit into something? Suanne takes out knitting needles and intentionally makes meaning out of what has happened to her. Ordinary experiences become a divine venue for recognizing what the "Stirring" is nudging her to receive and own.

The Sound of a Million Dreams explores the terrain of one life. This attention to life makes Suanne a credible cartographer for those with dreams of becoming and doing something in this world. On ancient maps perfect east was at the top—in God's heaven. The explored and unexplored world oriented around the Creator. Where human charting failed, at the edge of the known world, one often found the words "here be dragons." This lovely and courageous book journeys to edges of "here be dragons" and then to "here be dreams." Her compass points to perfect east—God at the top of the map giving her a world to enjoy and explore.

Walk with Suanne as she names things we all struggle to name and own and carry. Let her remembered life take you to the sacred and hidden heart of your dreams. Let her story give you courage to carry your dreams with intention and attention and "tireless endurance" right now.

I'm glad Suanne summoned up courage to become the kind of person who could birth a dream she longed to give the world. May the truth of her life in this lovely, delicious read help you *become the kind of person* that can do what is in your heart to do.

1

Ashes

Sometimes I don't know exactly what it is I want,
but it fairly makes my heart ache, I want it so.

MARK TWAIN

Two small scraps of paper weigh heavy in each pocket. One barely legible, scribbled in a hasty scrawl: *I am but dust.* The other bold, clear, strong—a canny invitation: *The world was made for me.*

My imagination turns over the old Hassidic proverb, the implications of each scrap twisting provocatively at the edges of my mind.

The first, our own finiteness, is true, indisputable. The beauty of it hit me square in the chest one year in the sacredness of a sanctuary where my friend Tracey taught me to dampen my thumb in a bowl laden with ashes and make the sign of the cross on a person's forehead. Each and every forehead.

Remember that you are dust, and to dust you will return.

For thirty minutes I said it, over and over again, as I stared into the dark and innocent eyes of a child; as I brushed my thumb across the oily pimples of a teenager; as I gently pressed the soft, dented wrinkles of an elderly woman; as I crossed the dark skin of a man in a narrow suit and tie and admired the flowing, unkempt curls of a young woman stooped forward in slouchy Australian boots. I crossed and I kneeled and I hugged and I blessed, recognizing each moment—diverse, unique, personal, communal—for the gift of redemption it was, as the tears streamed openly and unashamedly down my face.

There's beauty in dust.

The world was made for me.

The second is false. In fact, perhaps no more untrue and misleading statement has ever been made. The world was not made for me, neither for me individually nor for us collectively. The world was created by a flawless artist, a soulful creator, a stainless king, a triune spirit living in the perfect perichoresis of both genesis and eternity, who one day breathed life into this world, said it was not good until it was very good and then allowed it to flourish—and implode—time and time again, all as part of a long and twisted and redeeming love story. The world was not made for me, but I for it. Which is to say I for him.

There's beauty in this world.

How to embrace the tension, the endless possibilities of who we long to become ensconced between dust and eternity while still experiencing the beauty of both—before the nimble swing of the pendulum relentlessly threatens to knock us to the edges of the earth?

Now that really is the question we've all been asking since the first whispered breath.

Some days the bouncing of the train irritates my soul.

It's 7:55 a.m. and I'm on the Metra, plummeting into the heart of the city, Chicago that is.

Over the years, I've accepted the bouncing as normal, for the train does this as it finds its way down the tracks; it ebbs and flows, bobs and weaves—moving, swaying, floating—back and forth between the two rails, a bare-backed horse fidgety under the weight of its passengers. More often than not, I extend grace. But today my tolerance has flat-lined, and I'm beginning to feel the train is carrying, along with its passengers, a personal vendetta against my soul.

When we arrive at Union Station, I'll pack up my belongings, burrow into my down parka, effortfully sling my backpack across both shoulders and with one audible sigh make the long trek across the city, dodging and weaving its thousands of harried commuters until I arrive at my office, fifteen stories above the bustle composed of an ironic combination of ruthless ambition and barely limping by.

That's where my façade of being a competent grown-up begins.

It will hit me full force the moment I step into my office, but for now, for these next thirty-eight minutes on the train, I am the master of my own time. I alone decide each minute's fate and how I will invest in it: create, contemplate, meditate, pray, listen, rest, stare. Or simply be. I am grateful for the rare luxury of choice as my life outside this metal car fast approaches, the life in which I frenetically trade various cloaks of responsibility, sometimes within moments of one another: full-time employee, mother of two, wife of a work-laden husband, friend to a few life-giving souls; home-scheduler, bill-payer, endless kid-shuttle-er; forgetful scatterbrain, insecure mess, affirmation junkie; lover of the deep and meaningful, student of words, exercise addict, world-changer wannabe; writer, reader, teacher.

Believer.

Dreamer.

This morning, I choose to write. I sit with my laptop in the crook of my hips, legs crossed, and enjoy the gentle tapping that's become synonymous with the rhythm of my streaming consciousness, the flowing of ideological freedom, as words, when we really stop to think about it, magically appear before our eyes.

Only today the words don't come. They are stuck. Murky and slow, beetles drudging their way through sludge, struggling to inch their way toward the light they know will eventually come but that for now feels a million miles away.

Hoping to ease my growing anxiety, I become like a desperate hen scratching for grubs. Surely inspiration isn't entirely elusive. I pull out a few books from my backpack, dig my way through the pages of others, rummage through old computer files for words of my own. Close my eyes, search my mind intently. Hum. Twiddle. Wait for my soul to fill. I glance out the window, goading creation to loosen its grasp, to throw me a bone, but the sun is refracting off the fresh fallen snow so abnormally bright that its glare is offensive to my eyes.

I wait, but nothing happens. Today, the present remains painfully void.

So I lift my chin and look, instead, at the other end of the car where a middle-aged man wearing a black wool coat, collar pulled tight around his neck, faces me. He peers over the top of his sunglasses on this sub-zero February day, trolling his phone. His hair is short, crew-cut short, and I can't help but stare at the bald spot on the top of his head when he dips his chin. I wonder if the glare is offending him too.

All the while the train keeps bouncing, this time so violently I grab each side of my laptop to keep it from crashing into the train wall. Temptation settles in. Procrastination creeps. Frustration mounts.

Remember you are but dust.

I wonder vaguely if my irritation has nothing to do with the train and its bouncing. I wonder if today it's because the words, my current purpose in life, are stuck. Hopelessness tightens around my throat, water rising in an illusionist's tank with no hope of escape.

I hear the tempter spitting his sweet lies and the questions humankind has been asking throughout eternity; I sing in chorus with them today.

What am I doing here? Not just here, but Here?

The agitation of my surroundings, the sun glaring angrily at the corner of my right eye, the low rumble in the pit of my stomach, and the raw honesty of my finitude, of the ashes, suddenly makes me laugh at the sheer ridiculousness of the whole thing. I'm ready to put on the lightest of the cloaks and quit whatever it is I'm doing on this train.

But then I hear it again, dripping, a futile mixture of anticipation and disgust.

The world was made for you.

I scoff, at least at first. I hate the way this adage has become a heroine coursing through our cultural veins, a virtual IV drip that tempts us to believe that we're more important than we really are, that this world will tumble into oblivion unless we contribute our verse. But still, there's something alluring about the invitation, cornflower hyacinths blooming on a sweet spring day, and it makes me believe that something amazing is possible. It holds a sliver of truth, but one that only makes sense when we experience the world as a continuum into eternity, when we remember the truth of the redeeming love story and the paradox of the ashes.

And so instead of succumbing to despair, letting the pendulum knock me to the edge of the earth, I plead with God about what to do with the weight that presses hard in the middle of my chest, the alluring charm of the dreams that beckon me to make a dent in the world at the same time I fail to articulate exactly what they are. I ask him what to do with the rumblings inside that entice me to chase the future while still mandating that I be faithful to the present. I ask him about the truth of the continuum between dust and eternity, about my place in this world and where he would have me go. I listen. I contemplate the person I am and the one I someday want to become.

And I find myself wondering if I'm the only one who's ever sat on a train, sat anywhere, and wondered these things, who's ever been in the midst of hurtling toward their ordinary and busy life feeling like they were made for something that they couldn't quite put their finger on but that was, at the same time, one of the most pure and honest things they knew to be true.

The loudspeaker interrupts my thoughts. *Chi-cago, Union Station.*

The train doors open and I slip into the crowd, feeling the weight of the tiny scraps of paper in each pocket as I put one foot in front of the other all the way across the city.

2

The First Sound I Remember

We must learn to listen to the cock-crows and hammering and tick-tock of our lives for the holy and elusive word that is spoken to us out of their depths.

FREDERICK BUECHNER, *THE SACRED JOURNEY*

A person can think a long time about the first sound they ever heard and never come up with it.

Doctors say that babies can hear in utero between sixteen and eighteen weeks, most likely the sound of their mother's voice. I imagine those doctors are right, but I've thought a lot about that first sound with little success. Intuitively, I'm certain it was the sound of my mother's or father's voice, perhaps in the womb, the sound of one or both of them exclaiming when they first heard the news that they were expecting their fourth child. Maybe it was filled with excitement, maybe anxiety, or perhaps a mix of both. Two school teachers, a coach, an at-home mom trying to figure out how they were going to make ends meet. Or maybe they were just happy.

The harder I've tried to come up with it, the more convinced I've become that it's an impossible feat. Fortunately for us, most of life happens in the trying, and so in taking the time to listen, I've gained more time than I've lost. For in the process of listening for that one particular sound, I've heard a lot of others along the way.

And listening is no small thing.

The farm where I grew up is nestled in a small western Pennsylvanian town with two minor intersections. The first was a four-way stop in the middle of town where, according to the US Census Bureau, 151 people lived; it was the intersection just past the post office, the one that stopped shy of the playground with its fraying basketball nets and rusted chain-link fence, and the old white church in whose basement I first met Jesus. The other, a two-way stop on the far side of town, was known by everyone simply as "the Corners" and was home to the small family diner where I got my first job, the town's only gas station, and Beall and Nairn's motorcycle repair shop. My family's house sat on 275 acres—a mixture of dense woods, open pastures, and hay fields—on the opposite end of the township where my dad grew up with his parents and three younger brothers nearly sixty years before.

It's the sacred place where my story finds its beginning and where the sounds that continue to resound the most will always live:

The smack of an axe, the splintering of wood, the clunk of the freshly cut log hitting the woodpile as my dad, dressed in an old barn coat and his favorite navy beanie, labored to stack what would heat our house all winter long.

The snapping of green beans—crack, snip, snap—as my mom sat hunched over, brown paper bag at her feet, in the shade of the back porch, the one that sat adjacent to the L-shaped garden where summers were made, a cornucopia of tomatoes and cabbage and corn and broccoli and watermelon and pumpkins that us kids had seeded ourselves.

The crunch of gravel as a car wound long and slow up our steep Pennsylvania drive, the engine echoing through the hollow of the hills, the dogs, strays turned kin, running to the top of the yard, stopping at the cascading willow, smiling through their barks as the car neared the house.

The soft scraping of the front door, the one that no one outside the family and a few close friends could ever open on the first try, their thumbs pressing the black plastic handle and pulling too quickly—once, twice, three times—before the latch would finally unleash and the rubber along the bottom of the door brushed the concrete step of the porch.

The buzz of the electric box in the basement, whose bright red light was the only thing that lit up its concrete walls and tiny windows that barely pushed above the hard earth, letting us know that the electric fence circling the cow pasture was on.

The sizzling of the electric skillet on a lazy Sunday afternoon, the smell of fried chicken, gravy, and rice wafting through the house as the muffled sounds of the Steelers' game drifted up the step into the kitchen from the family room TV.

The gasp of my mother's voice the day she opened the front door, me bumping into her heels eager to be home after a long day at school, and stared into the vacant countertop that had once held our microwave, the first sign we'd been robbed.

The soothing melody of "Angel of the Morning" blaring from the boom box inside my brother's bedroom the day my grandma died.

Later there were sounds of sports and heartbreaks and friends and weddings and jobs, but it's the early sounds that help us find the beginning of our stories—the sounds that start weaving together the picture of who we were and who we've become, the ones that sweetly hand us a snapshot of ourselves that we otherwise may have forgotten. For these are the sounds that lead us into the sounds of our lives.

Sounds have a unique way of sticking in our minds, transporting us to a time and space that brings with it memories and emotions of that which was. Sometimes one blends into another, one snapshot leading to the next, making it impossible to distinguish where one sound ends and another begins. Others stand out, distinct photographs that, without warning, put a lump in our throat, making us pause long enough to pull them out of the messy pile and set them aside, a treasure we come back to again and again. Listening for these sounds takes time, but the more we listen, the more we let our imaginations work and play, the better chance we have of arranging the pieces of the puzzle with all their straight edges, mismatched sizes, and peeled cardboard corners that little by little reveal the people we were created to be and the ones we continue to become. This is where our stories start to pick up steam, because revealing the pieces of who we are and what we want to become is one of the great sojourns of life.

Listening to sounds with more than just our ears. That's how Pulitzer Prize–nominated author Frederick Buechner describes it in his memoir *The Sacred Journey*. "They were all of them random sounds without any apparent purpose or meaning and yet as I paused to listen to them, I found myself hearing them with something more than just my ears to the point where they became in some way enormously meaningful."

Enormously meaningful.

In the months after the doctors say our ears begin to hear, there will be a myriad of sounds that rush around us before we ever even realize we can hear them—sounds that jump, swirl, and crawl into our lives, seeping into our psyches both because of and in spite of ourselves and which make the words of Barbara Brown Taylor all the more profound: "The practice of paying attention," she says, "really does take time. Most of us move so quickly that our surroundings become no more than the blurred scenery we fly past on our way to somewhere else."

Now doesn't that sound like a shame?

And so paying attention takes practice and intentionality and patience for which we need to take time, time to stop rushing and running by all of the chaos and clamor and listen to the sounds that have made us who we are; sounds that are holy and sacred music, teaching us where we belong in this world and to whom we first and foremost belong. They reveal our character, our giftedness, our limitations, our values, and the deep-seeded dreams that God has so tenderly placed inside our hearts. They wake us to the deepest places in our souls and call us by name.

But perhaps the sounds that scream at us loudest are the ones that often come to us in the most quiet, giving us a window into who we really are, at night when no one is looking, when we're afraid to tell anyone what whispers inside of us; the ones that beckon and inspire us to make our own song. We battle fear and insecurity and self-doubt and loathing, but we also dare to believe that life isn't random, that these sounds have been woven together for a purpose: to give us clues into who we are and what we are to do with this one life we've been given. It's part of all of our stories as we make our way through this world trying to give to it, and leave with it, a portion of who we are.

The first time the sound of a dream slammed, hard, in the center of my spirit was almost a decade ago. It's the sound that has led me on the journey whose threads are pulled through this book, an intimate pilgrimage, often ironically nomadic, that I've struggled to comprehend; it's been unlike anything else I've ever known. It happened in a coffee shop during my thirtieth year, and in less than two hours it caused me to listen to my life anew. The sounds I heard that day and the ones I took the time to listen to from my past would converge, creating a mosaic of desire and doubt that would begin an evolution in my soul, a relentless pursuit of a God who would woo me, gently and kindly, to offer myself to the world as a way to sanctify the person he wanted me to become.

I've been paying attention ever since.

3

In the Meantime

*There is no passion to be found playing
small—in settling for a life that is less than
the one you are capable of living.*

NELSON MANDELA

I sat in a leather chair, opposite my favorite college professor,
and stared at him in disbelief.

An internship? Seriously? A graduation requirement?

It was the spring of my junior year, and I had fallen madly in
love with a lean and handsome college baseball player two years my
senior. I met Eric two years before, sitting knee-to-knee in a prayer
circle, and was forever changed when his deep tenor prayed tenderness over a girlfriend two hundred miles away. It's a piece of our
story that always sounds more pious than it actually was, but still
a profound moment in my spiritual life. I had never before con-
sidered that there were boys who prayed for girls. I had no idea this
was a thing. But I instantly knew I wanted one.

One October evening, about a year after our knees first touched,
Eric and I stood in the glow of the fluorescent light outside my

dorm, cobbled brick cold under our feet, where, for the dozenth time, he asked me to dinner. I was still devising a plan to break things off with my long-standing high school boyfriend, and so, for the dozenth time, I turned him down. He leaned in close, his tall frame bending over mine. *Don't worry*, he whispered in the tip of my ear, *I'm not going anywhere.*

That was it. I floated up four stories, flopped on my dorm room bed, and in a dramatic, movie-style fashion, announced to my roommate I found the man I was going to marry. Our relationship progressed quickly, and now, more than a year later, Eric had signed as a free agent with the New York Yankees. As I sat in my professor's office, I hadn't seen him in almost four months, an epic amount of time for a sappy-eyed teenager in the days when email was barely comprehensible; calling card rates dictated our most valued exchanges. I already had plans to spend the summer watching him live out his dream in Greensboro, North Carolina. The manager at Applebee's had promised me a job.

I was supposed to have an internship?

My mind frantically searched for some sort of knowing: A meeting with my advisor? A requirement list someone had given me? Conversations with other journalism students? A childhood flashback flooded my mind, a knowing inadequacy rising in the back of my throat: Ms. Peters's kindergarten class. Standing in line at the chalkboard, waiting my turn as the class worked through their ABCs. I was the only one who didn't know each and every one.

Seriously? An internship?

The fact that my professor loved baseball as much as he loved teaching ended up being my saving grace. Rather than giving me the scolding I deserved, he made a few calls, now it seems with almost a twinkle in his eye. I spent my summer in North Carolina, a baseball groupie working at a diner, and completed my internship for the university that fall. It was the summer of Eric's first injury, his first hitting slump, and the one in which we got engaged.

We got married the fall after I graduated (his three-year minor league career at an abrupt end due to an unfortunate injury) and spent several fun years in Pittsburgh as DINKS (Dual Income No Kids), which meant we had a lot of money and virtually no adult responsibilities. We'd meet downtown for lunch, play racquetball in the evenings at the local YMCA, and drive out to the Farm for Saturday night hamburgers, a welcome tradition despite the fact I never actually liked the burgers. We adopted a coonhound named Jake who lived with us for four months until his incessant barking and ruthless hole digging nearly got us kicked out of our rental. (I eventually dropped him off at the Farm on a weekend my parents were away and waited to tell them until they came home, a fact I still feel mortified about to this day.) We joined an eclectic little church, a hundred-some-person congregation that manifested community in such a compelling way that it would later alter Eric's own vocational journey and become a core of our married life.

During these early years, I held three different jobs. My first after college was as the manager of a desktop-publishing section of a copy store. I fired my first person, a shy young redhead who was so skinny I thought the wind might blow him over and who, if I had to do it over again, rather than suggest we let him go, I would choose compassion for, take under my wing, and pull out of his shell. The second job was as a community relations manager at a national bookstore chain, a job I quit on the spot after months of being bullied by an assistant manager who once told me my desk looked like a college dorm room (in hindsight she was probably right), and the third at a public relations firm that served only high-tech clients, because you could actually have a thriving business doing this in the late nineties.

It was at the public relations firm that I got my first sizable clue, although I wouldn't recognize it at the time, into what would take me two decades to accept about myself. My boss, who was also the owner and founder of the small start-up, was conducting my performance review. When he got to a section about analytics and strategy and organizational skills, my scores plummeted. He explained to me, as gently as he could, that while there were things I did well, these were not among them. I was embarrassed, this time inadequacy showing in the red of my face, tears stinging the corners of my eyes. I hadn't yet learned that people are wired in different ways, that not only was it okay to be strong in some areas and limited (or downright awful) in others, it was perfectly normal. In fact, it was an intricacy that kept the world from falling into an abyss of boredom, a whimsical truth that helped make the world go round. It would take years for me to accept this truth, to freely celebrate the gifts of others while simultaneously admitting, without being swallowed into the bowels of inadequacy, that they weren't my own, to stop pretending that there were things I could do well when it was obvious to everyone around me that clearly I could not, to stop apologizing for my limitations and instead embrace the artistry of a world that needs every good thing we carry equally, one not better than the other, no one less than.

I'd later read a book by Os Guinness titled *The Call* in which he admonishes his readers to "do what you are." Meaning don't simply find a job or invest your time into areas that check off a list of boxes that you're merely good at (or not so good at) or even educated for; invest your time into the areas where God truly calls you into his kingdom, where the interior of who you are aligns with the exterior of a cosmos in which you have no choice but to spend eons of your time. Instead of living by this truth, I'd spend the next segment of my life trying to figure out how to align these pieces of myself through work, a recurring pattern, ending up in jobs that

I felt like I should be good at or wanted to be good at but never really fit who I was. It wasn't until the Stirring that I'd start to recognize I had it all wrong.

After three years in Pittsburgh, Eric and I would stand in front of our eclectic little church and say one of the hardest goodbyes we'd ever have to say. We'd move to Ohio, one town away from Eric's parents, and spend the next three years as missionaries, our summers spent traveling abroad. I'd write a few articles for the ministry's magazine, the first draft of which my editor would redline almost in its entirety. Eric would learn his real passion and calling was for the church, and he'd eventually transition from missionary to pastor. We'd have two kids fifteen months apart (the reason we never had a third), scrape enough money together to buy our first house and a minivan: signs that we were inescapably and fully adults. I would spend my days at home with my children and wonder what I was supposed to be doing with my life.

I'd sit in the deep recesses of my professor's chair and wonder if everyone had figured it out but me.

4

Stirrings

It is, I think, that we are all so alone in what lies deepest in our souls, so unable to find the words, and perhaps the courage to speak with unlocked hearts, that we don't know at all that it is the same with others.

SHELDON VANAUKEN, *A SEVERE MERCY*

The best thing about moving is that you get to start over. One morning, you get to wake up and reinvent your life, a clean slate to do what you want to do and be who you want to be. Except the truth about reinventing your life is that you tend to reinvent the same person you've always been with the same life you've always had because you don't really know how to be anybody but who you are. If you're lucky, maybe a few small changes will creep into your routine, a character trait will stick, a few new boundaries will hold.

Or maybe something really profound will happen. Maybe just one small change will last, a drip-drop of a sound whose ripples will carry a sliver of who you are right into the satin mist of heaven.

For me, it started with the stomach flu.

I remember three things about that day: I had just recovered from the stomach flu; I had stolen Eric's laptop (it would be years before I could afford my own), and I sat on a hard wooden chair.

We had moved to Chicago just a few months before, a move that was oddly anticipated at the same time it was completely unforeseen. For reasons neither of us could put our fingers on, for months before the move we were living with the faint and unsettled feeling that change was coming, that maybe God had something different in mind than the life we'd been living. Looking back, I think God's kindness alone was the netting that prepared us for the upheaval that would soon come.

It began with an out-of-the-blue email I'd read for the first of a dozen times sitting on the steps of our Ohio deck, the deck Eric built with my brother over a sticky Fourth of July weekend in between premarital counseling sessions and bottles of icy cold beer. As I often did during those early years, I sat on the edge of the wooden planks watching my pasty-legged, German-English-descended toddlers, Sadie and Clay, run up and down the small tree-lined hill in the backyard, taking turns pushing one another on the black plastic truck with the broken trunk that we'd accosted from the neighbor. Eric handed me the email that now rested in my hands. Every few paragraphs my eyes lifted to the kids, a now natural and often habit, taking in the budding green from the cornfield that rested on the other side of the shallow tree line, while Eric's broad shadow covered mine. *Waiting.*

Although the email was a simple invitation to explore a possibility (*Dear Eric, I received your name from a professor in your graduate school. He thought you might be interested in this position . . .*), I knew this was the change we'd subconsciously been waiting for. With a wisp of the breeze, I knew that the pieces of our lives were about to be drastically rearranged, not in the dramatic fashion caused by a terminal illness or a tragic accident or some awful and unexpected crisis, but enough of a tousle that it would be a while before we'd find our balance again.

Six months later (and, thanks to the stress, ten pounds lighter), we watched snow-covered soybeans and cornfields turn into concrete highways and crowded strip malls. Exactly three days before Christmas, we pulled into a neighborhood of towering elms and fenced-in yards, slapped up a twenty-five-dollar Walmart Christmas tree, kicked up our feet and wondered how this new life would unfold.

We were in a city of nine million souls—and didn't know a single one.

The stomach flu was a bad one.

Eric was sick. Clay was sick. Sadie had just gotten done being sick. It was the eighth time we'd had the stomach flu in four years, one of the many initiations into parenthood that people fail to mention when they're gushing over your swaddled newborn. It had been four years of living with two toddlers who were three months short of being Irish Twins. Four years since I quit my job, four years since I'd had an uninterrupted night of sleep, four years since I'd spent more money on any slinky dress hanging in my closet than on diapers. Four years since I'd been alone in my house, since I'd thought about something more than how I was going to make it through the day without losing my temper or taking a nap. Four years and I was still overwhelmed by the dense fog that covers you when your children are very young, the one that makes you feel like every day is the longest day you've ever lived.

I looked between Eric moaning on one couch, Clay asleep on the other, and knew that some moments, no matter how selfish, were meant to be seized.

It had been three months since we heaved the Walmart Christmas tree up the attic steps. I was exhausted, overwhelmed, and, for the first time in my life, lonely. Seriously, intensely lonely. Something inside of me was sinking slowly and deeply under water, creating the kind of muffled gurgling I've come to recognize when a person's soul fails to come up for air. The combination of being desperate to escape and being fortunate enough to be the first one to shake the nasty bug provided me a rare sliver of an opportunity to be alone. A better woman would have tended to the wounded, maybe scrubbed a toilet and bleached some doorknobs, but my desperation sighed louder than any moaning that came from the couch. I tucked Eric's laptop under one arm, pushed my coat under the other, and, before regret could make an appearance, dashed for the car.

I vaguely knew what I was running for.

My desire was to write. I had the edges of a memory floating in my mind for the better part of these four years, a simple vignette whose nuances I was itching to play with, a puppy set free from the confines of a gated room. I wasn't sure what I wanted to do with it exactly, but I was curious to see what would happen if I allowed myself to tap into its subtleties, what mysteries lay within that were waiting to be teased out. Most importantly, like all stories, I wanted to see what would happen once it stepped into this world and caught its first breath. And so I found myself in a coffee shop—105 deep-breathing minutes without interruption—with a computer at my fingertips, a hot cup of coffee in my hand, and a vintage snapshot dancing through my head.

I broke the surface of the water and inhaled fresh air. I let my imagination roam and remembered what it was like for my mind to be free, to create without limits, to explore a piece of myself that had gotten lost in life and work and diapers and dishes and dried milk and dirty socks, a piece that had gotten sucked into the timeless vacuum, as many of our pieces do, by the myriad chores of life. Only it was more than a familiar piece that had gotten lost; it was a piece I'm not sure I ever knew existed. It was a piece that was waiting to become.

I wish I could tell you that what lay before me at the end of that hour and forty-five minutes was an act of creative genius, that the work in and of itself was some kind of epiphany, but I can't even come close. In fact, I'm certain the execution of my craft was quite poor. But as it turns out, it wasn't what came out of me that was significant that day, but what entered in. For right in the middle of that very ordinary day, inside that very suburban coffee shop, on that very hard wooden chair, the presence of God entered my dreams. My soul lurched with a longing so intense that I did a quick scan of the tables to see if anyone else noticed the shift in the room—but no one had so much as fluttered an eyelash. Perhaps it was the first time in four years that I wrote a story down, but it was the first time in my life that I felt the Stirring.

Putting it into words—the Stirring, that is—is no easy task, especially when it happens in something as complicated as a person's soul. Definition, in fact, threatens to cheapen the experience, like trying to explain the way the crimson of the sun dipping below the ocean makes your chest cavity fill as you wiggle your toes into the damp of the sand or the way the breath of a child warm against your neck leaks contentment through your every pore or the way the right person's hand in yours makes every speck of the galaxy fall magically, peacefully into place.

But if I had to, if I had to try to explain, I'd say the Stirring was a moment: an awareness of the holy in the midst of the everyday that simultaneously brought clarity and chaos to my space in the world. A feeling: a perpetual pressing, pushing, and pulling that happened and continues to happen all at once, a mystery not unlike the way we say the kingdom of God is both now and not yet, both here and yet to come, both within us and among us, that was compelling me to *do* something. A vision: a pathway for the future whose specifics I couldn't catch sight of but was certain existed nonetheless. A longing: an ache to offer a piece of myself to the world that held within it the smallest hope of leaving a mark. An invitation: a solicitation to view life through a new lens, a kindling that burned so deeply I'd spend the next ten years trying to figure it out.

A calling.

A dream.

A gift.

For the first time since I'd been floundering through my early professional life and motherhood, my soul aligned in such a way that something about myself finally made sense; the sounds of my life trickled through time in an entirely new arrangement. And my soul lurched again: there was something more than my present that life was beckoning me to. There was something I was supposed to do. There was a person I was supposed to become.

In the days moving forward, when someone asked me about the Stirring, I couldn't find words to describe it; my throat constricted and I felt as if I might cry for reasons that, to this day, I can't exactly explain. "This is something I can't not do, for reasons I'm unable to explain to anyone else and don't fully understand myself but that are nonetheless compelling," says Parker Palmer. Yes, it's something like that.

If only I knew what exactly the "something" was.

I found myself wondering if I was alone in the Stirring, much like the way I felt alone when I first moved to Chicago, watching billions of people buzzing around, convinced that they all knew one another, knew each other's stories, had been to one another's houses and had built decks together over bottles of icy cold beer, reclining in lounge chairs as they swapped stories about the meaning of life—and that I was the only one left out.

And I found myself wondering if I was somehow supposed to know what to do with this weight that landed so solidly in my chest that, in the days to come, it would become a permanent companion, never relenting its poking and prodding, not even during the most chaotic moments of my most hectic days.

The uncertainty it elicited reminded me of the day I left the hospital with Sadie, my firstborn child. The nurses put me in a wheelchair, placed a swaddled newborn in my arms, and then pushed me out the sliding doors with barely a wave goodbye. All I kept thinking was how I couldn't believe they were really going to let me leave with another actual person—one with whom I actually had no idea what to do. Sometime later, it would dawn on me that this is how parents have felt throughout time and I'd guess how most of us feel as we move throughout life. We put one foot in front of the other, beg God for mercy, and do the best we can.

I'd like to ask God to explain the Stirring to me someday, whenever my someday comes (as if he and I could have a long conversation about it), but I've learned to cry "mystery" the way a child learns to cry "uncle." I've reasoned enough of it away and have ached with regret that I've learned, instead of always searching for firm answers, to trust the nudges and nigglings that stir in my spirit—especially when it comes to my dreams—and to offer myself fully to them, not reserving the crumbs for another space in time that may or may not come, even when comprehension feels elusive, doubt massive, and to risk following their tracks through the dark of the forest as an act of obedience and faith. I've found it better to live this way, a life that grants the humility and freedom to admit that I was wrong rather than never to try at all. That's the way it should be with dreams.

And so writing became a conduit to my dreams, a portal through which the holy entered and changed the person I was to become. For a long time, I would make the mistake of thinking the holiness was about the writing itself, but that only goes to show how often we desire our life to be about the tangible things we achieve instead of accepting that most of our tangibles are simply vehicles to becoming who we were always meant to be. This, as it turns out, would become the most important thing about the Stirring. For our dreams are never meant to be an end in and of themselves.

I came home from the coffee shop and announced to my still-moaning family that something profound and mysterious had happened to me.

No one paid much attention.

But I knew I would never be the same.

5

Be When I Grow Up

*We begin to find and become ourselves when we notice
how we are already found, already truly, entirely, wildly,
messily, marvelously who we were born to be.*

ANNE LAMOTT, "HOW TO BECOME THE
PERSON YOU WERE MEANT TO BE"

It's a cold December afternoon. I am sitting in one of my favorite coffee shops, next to the train station, next to the bay window encased in honey-stained oak that leaves a quaint view of the winter's first snowfall. It's been more than a year since the Stirring. I now have a laptop that, for the first time, I can call my own, a refurbished hunk passed on by my friend Andy, a business owner who was updating his company's stock. ("We have tons of them we don't use," he'd said.) So I'd started sitting in lots of coffee shops, an at-home mom trying to find her way, my kids now safely tucked away in school for most of my day.

Although I can see the bricked shops that line the other side of the street, the sill, resting slightly higher than my right shoulder, cuts the buildings in a horizontal midline. The snow is falling lazily as it makes its way to the ground, but every now and then its path is redirected by a microburst of wind. The branches of an evergreen wreath gently tap the glass in rhythm with the breeze. The back of a parking meter is slicked wet and black, causing the snow to stick and then hang, resembling a strip of Santa's beard, nature's way of not being outdone by the velvet of any crimson bow.

For a while, I can't take my eyes off a red string that's gotten itself hopelessly tangled in the prickly branches of the tree across the street, perhaps a string to a child's lost balloon. I glance at an advertisement for a new meatball pesto flatbread and wrinkle my nose at the thought of eating it with my coffee.

There are three parking spots within my view: the one in the front and back, both occupied by oversized, black SUVs, are stagnate, but the one in the middle has had a revolving array of occupants, and I find myself curious about who these people are. Where they might be going on such a cold winter day, what life they may have waiting for them after they pull out of the spot. A business executive with a demanding job and a boss he hates, a mom trying to squeeze in a few more errands before she picks up the kids from school, an exasperated caretaker with an elderly parent waiting for a prescription, a carpenter fixing the store's leaky plumbing, a woman who's so bored with her own life that she's hoping another swipe of the credit card might fill the emptiness lingering in her soul.

For a long time the spot remains empty. A white pickup truck passes slowly, the words "Gourmet's Choice" centered on the passenger side door. A gold suburban brakes momentarily but then moves on, having decided that eking out a parallel park might be more than he can handle. Maybe all those passing by decide the space is too tight, too hard to squeeze into. Maybe cars filled with people who feel like that string caught in the tree, too tangled to get loose.

I wonder if they like their life. I wonder if they are living the life they thought they'd be.

When I was young, I'm not sure what I would have told you I wanted to be when I grew up. It was a million things, and it was nothing at all.

Somewhere around the age of eight, I built an entire detective agency in my parents' basement. My granddad's black walnut desk, salvaged from the farmhouse where my dad grew up, sat on the cold concrete floor. It was the hardest piece of furniture you'd ever felt, a block of granite bending the fingers of earth, and was the perfect center for my business. The accordion roll top hid a myriad of compartments and hard-to-see crevices, so many nooks and crannies that the possibilities of function were endless. To top it off, my mom's part-time job as the township secretary gave me access to an old typewriter (complete with an erasable ink cartridge), a seal press, receipt book, and titanic-sized stapler. It was an imagination's dream.

In eighth grade I thought I might take up acting. I think this one stuck for a little while, even landed me the lead in my senior high play, an awkward murder mystery in which I—the Sandy Olsson of my class—wore a tight little black skirt and hung a cigarette out of the corner of my mouth. Other than the somewhat amazing, yet bizarrely odd, talent of my male counterpart (who once sent me a series of secret love notes that culminated in the words "you are my oxygen," talked like Christian Slater, and later made a movie of his own), I'm pretty sure the whole thing was a disaster.

Around sixteen I decided a marine biologist might be fun, mostly because I wanted to swim with dolphins at Sea World. Because, let's face it—who didn't?

What I never would have told you I wanted to be was a writer. In fact, I'm one of the few writers I know who never dreamed of winning a third-grade essay contest or whose professional credits doesn't include a miserable whodunit novel penned in junior high. I was too busy playing football in the front yard with my brothers and skinning up my knees on my bike. And, of course, I was, after all, very busy with the detective agency.

What's more, I've always found writing to be incredibly difficult, a painfully slow and arduous process that's not unlike trying to get to the gym after you've been lying on the couch eating Cheetos and binging on Netflix for six months, or having sex at 11:00 p.m. when you've already been up since five. The irony of such conflicts is that you know you'll feel good about your accomplishment once you've followed through—*you will be so proud of yourself*—but getting yourself to commit in the moment feels equivalent to leaping a tall building on a pogo stick. And because writing is that way for me, because it's so difficult, I find myself skeptical of those who can write quickly or without feeling the need to bare their soul on every page. In fact, I find myself skeptical of people who walk through life this way; for something to really matter, I feel it should cause a certain amount of pain. I feel that, at least sometimes, life should be as hard for everyone as writing is for me.

"Now when some people sit down to write and nothing special comes, no good ideas," says Brenda Ueland in her book *If You Want to Write*, "they are so frightened that they drink a lot of strong coffee to hurry them up, or smoke packages of cigarettes, or take drugs or get drunk. They do not know that good ideas come slowly and that the more clear, tranquil and unstimulated you are, the slower the ideas come but the better they are." That makes me feel better. Because I am so slow. Not just at writing, but at life.

In any case, answering what you want to be when you grow up is a complex and difficult task. I've never had much luck figuring it out myself, and have found that, after badgering others with incessant questions and waiting for whimsical and magic answers that never came, only a rare and lucky few have had any better fortune than me.

When I needed a break from building the booming detective business in my parents' basement, I'd come upstairs to our green shag living room carpet and get lost in stacks of my mom's 45 records. She had hundreds of them, kept in the bottom of a tall laminate cabinet in the living room (in pink, blue, yellow plastic cylinders with a lid and a handle), the same room where the turntable was.

My brother David and I spent hours dancing to Eddie Rabbit's "I Love a Rainy Night," J. Geils Band's "Freeze Frame" (although the lesser known side B, "Rage in the Cage," was our very favorite), White Snake's "Here I Go Again," Olivia Newton John's "Physical," and, heavens only knows why, anything sung by Kiss. We'd put on long black wigs and masks that smelled like the hard plastic they were made of (the kind that nick your tongue when you stuck it through the sliver of a mouth slit), and we'd rock out with Gene Simmons to "Rock n' Roll All Nite" and "I Was Made for Lovin' You." Our parents must have been too tired to care.

When David got bored of the dancing, he'd trot off to play Atari, and I'd collapse to the floor, cross-legged, and plunge into the stories, the ones whose narration and songs you'd follow along in the accompanying book: *Lady and the Tramp, The Jungle Book, The Fox and the Hound* (all profoundly tragic, by the way). But the story that most captivated me, the one I'd listen to over and over, was the story of *Tina the Ballerina*. Released in 1953 by Peter Pan records from the Tinkerbell LP, it was the story of a child who had a dream.

I'd pull the vinyl out of its thin cardboard sleeve and drop it, gently, carefully, on the turntable. I'd lay on my back and wait for the needle to drop, reveling in the anticipatory sounds: the click of the arm, the record gaining speed, the soft crunch of the needle as it caressed the record's surface, and then, the climactic static that meant the story was about to begin.

Once there was a little girl who loved to dance more than anything in the world. When Tina heard music, she would stop to dance. She would stand on her toes, stretch out her arms gracefully, and being to whirl around and around.

Tina . . . knew exactly what she wanted to be when she grew up. She would sit in the garden every day and think to herself: when I grow up, I want to be, a lovely ballerina. Wait and see, someday I'll be, a famous ballerina.

As the story goes on, Tina travels to the Paris ballet with her brother Jacques and finds herself in the audience front and center when the music comes to an abrupt stop. A man walks onto stage and announces that the star ballerina can no longer dance and so the ballet cannot continue. Tina jumps to her feet.

"Wait, wait sir!" Tina said. "I will dance in her place!"

"You, dance in the star ballerina's place? But you are such a little girl."

Then before anyone could stop her, Tina ran onto the stage and began to dance.

Round and round and round she goes.

Dancing, dancing on her toes.

Tina the Ballerina, the belle of old Paris (Par-eee).

Twirling, twirling in the spin, whirling, whirling like the wind.

Tina the Ballerina.

Tina danced and danced until she could dance no more.

I listened to that record ad nauseam. And for reasons I now cannot even fathom, I would dress up in my sister's pink sequined tutu and make my family sit on the green shag and watch, repeatedly, as I acted out the story of Tina the Ballerina.

The irony is palpable.

I've spent many adult moments wondering why I—a tomboy, a girl who built forts in the woods and ran barefoot through the soft mud of the creek and played hours of football in the yard with her brothers—was so taken with Tina the Ballerina. What is it that pulls us back to certain memories, songs, and smells? At the time it made no sense, but it does now, like so many things with years and experience and reflection and insight. I think when dreams unfold, when you start to step into them, you begin to learn and reflect on a lot about yourself—where you've come from, the memories that have made you who you are, memories in which you only find significance when you step back in time and replay them frame by frame, moment by moment, meaning by meaning.

I think God was speaking into who I was and who I'd become, even at that early (and awkward) age. Not specifically about anything I was to do, but rather into a piece of myself he knew would continually need to be reminded of the freedom that is found when one offers herself fully to her dreams, of the courage and confidence it requires, of the intentionality and tireless endurance it takes—and, paramount, of the importance of simply enjoying the pleasure of the dance.

He begins whispering to us, even as small children, through the infantile and profound, subtle and cataclysmic, the overt and the transparent, putting one bead on the bracelet at a time, leading us down a path we can't see before we even know there is a path to be on or which way it will lead. Like he spoke to Abram about going to a land he'd never seen and Moses about going back to Egypt and Philip about walking along a road with no more direction than "go south," he doesn't wait until we're ready to speak to us; he doesn't wait for us to arrive or to have it all figured out in order to fully become the people he always intended for us to be.

So what do you want to be when you grow up?

It's a timeless question.

It's a question we pause to ask ourselves at various points in our lives, but even in our most earnest attempts to figure it out, life has a way of needing us, and we think, *Now that's a good question to ponder. I'll come back to that when I have a little more time.* We search. We do things we don't really want to do. We struggle out of fear and doubt and insecurity. We get tossed like the wind between things that seemed like a good idea at the time or were the right (or only) thing at the time or that pay the bills or that are good for our family, but in the midst of it, ten or twenty or thirty years later, we realize we've lost sight of the very question we started out believing we'd find an answer to all along. And the years march on, and every once in a while the question flashes through our mind and we realize we've never really answered it. We pull in and out of the parking spot tired, exhausted, and overwhelmed, wondering if the space we're living in is a good fit or if the scenery will ever change.

So what do you want to be when you grow up?

We ask this question flippantly and patronizingly to children in elementary school. We ask teenagers as they prepare for college, college graduates as they prepare for careers, young adults as they prepare for families and buy their first house and move from the city to the suburbs; we ask mid-life-crises folks when they wonder if they should switch jobs, the last-third folks who are heading into retirement: *What do you want to be when you grow up?* It's like all of life has been working together in one chaotic vortex to move us in this one unknown and confusing direction since the time we were very young.

But in all of our flippancy, we don't often realize that we're asking one of the scariest and most difficult questions of all, because at its heart lies some very deep and soul-searching questions about who we are, who created us (and why), what we're passionate about, what we're gifted at, what we believe we have to offer the world, how we want to make a difference, and where we're invited to serve the kingdom of God in all its goodness. And, of course, there's always the fear that, in the end, when our casket is being lowered into the ground, we never figured it out. We simply wasted a lot of time.

But it's so much more than what we want to be when we grow up—an occupation we'd like to hold; it's about what lives and breathes and stirs passion inside each of us that longs to come out, to be heard, in a way that is wholly and uniquely each of us. It's about what God is saying to us when we listen to the sounds of our lives. It's about offering all of ourselves to the world. And not just as a way to offer ourselves to the world, but for the world to receive us in such a way that, when all is said and done, both we and it are never the same.

Maybe we need to stop forcing people to answer the question and, instead, invite them to spend more time listening to their lives, to create moments where their own Stirring can inhabit their soul and invite them to look at their lives anew, spaces where they can see the pieces of themselves that have been lost, and rediscover parts that were never meant to be buried so deeply under trying so hard to figure out what they were supposed to do when they grew up. Maybe we need to stop asking so many questions and, instead, sit in the presence of holiness, offering ourselves to it until we remember that we are but dust and that holiness invited us to be part of the world.

In her book *An Altar in the World*, Barbara Brown Taylor says this: "Earlier in my life, I thought there was one particular thing I was supposed to do with my life. I thought that God had a purpose for me and my main job was to discover what it was." She goes on to describe watching those with whom she graduated land jobs left and right while she continued to struggle to find her place. Like I would find myself doing, incessantly, after the Stirring, she began begging God to tell her what she was supposed to do when she grew up, what her designated purpose on this earth was supposed to be.

One night, she found herself pleading with God on a fire escape, hanging precariously from the side of a building, where she says she "learned to pray the way a wolf howls."

She describes her conversation with God.

> Then one night when my whole heart was open to hearing from God what I was supposed to do with my life, God said, "Anything that pleases you."
>
> "What?" I said, resorting to words again. "What kind of an answer is that?"
>
> "Do anything that pleases you," the voice in my head said again, "and belong to me."
>
> At one level, that answer was no help at all. The ball was back in my court again, where God had left me all kinds of room to lob it wherever I wanted. I could be a priest or a circus worker. God really did not care. At another level, I was so relieved that I sledded down the stairs that night. Whatever I decided to do for a living, it was not what I did but how I did it that mattered. God had suggested an overall purpose, but was not going to supply the particulars for me. If I wanted a life of meaning, then I was going to have to apply the purpose for myself.

God was not going to supply the particulars.

Purpose, after all, is not particular. Peculiar as it may be, purpose is not a result of any choice we make, for God alone purposes. Purpose is the aftershock of a God who is good, who postures his people toward his goodness, to know and experience more of his character and refract all that we absorb into the lives of others.

Purpose, therefore, actually precedes the particulars. Maybe we waste too much time trying to decipher the particulars.

I thought once again of Tina—standing with her arms extended, whirling and twirling in the beauty of the garden, the pleasure of her creator watching her dance as she offered herself to him and to the world—and reveled in its glory.

6

Picture Frames

When we think back on our life, we remember less
than half of it. The best we get is picture frames,
snapshots, scenes of moments as we go.

Donald Miller

y dad tells a story of when he was a kid.

He and his family sat in a small church parking lot where they often worshiped on Sunday mornings. They sat in the car waiting, for what I'm not sure, perhaps for the church doors to open, when the pastor drove up in an interminable white Cadillac. My dad admits he didn't know all that much about the Bible, but was pretty sure that Jesus had a lot to say about humility. After all, humility had wriggled its way into my dad's soul by osmosis through the story of his own father, the valedictorian of his high school who went off to college with aspirations to be a doctor; when the Depression hit, he was forced to drop out and was now a foreman at the local steel mill. A pastor driving a Cadillac seemed to him, even at a young age, a first-class show of hypocrisy.

He never forgot the way that made him feel, and as he recounts the story from the muted green of his living room chair, nearly sixty years later, even he is surprised how the image still sits unsettled, a termite waggling in his conscience. I ask him if that scene has affected his view of God, that maybe God wasn't really good or fair, or that he didn't care as much about my dad's hard-working, blue-collar family as he did that pastor. Or if maybe he felt like I imagine I would have, that the pastor was rubbing it—whatever *it* was—in their faces. *I don't think so*, he said. Whatever the case, my dad knew Jesus called his people to live better lives than that. He knew that Jesus himself was better than that.

Pastor Stern. That's what I thought his name was.

It was in the cold concrete walls of my best friend's church that I first met him, the white church across from the rusty-fenced basketball courts. I sat across from him on a cold, metal folding chair in a small dungeon of a room. It was during vacation Bible school, and us kids had taken a break from the kickball game in the gravel parking lot to refuel on vanilla cookies and a sticky red punch that tasted more like a cherry snow cone than an actual drink. Someone tapped me on the shoulder and told me it was my turn to go to the basement to talk to the pastor, and so off I went. The drop in temperature as I descended the red velvet stairs was palpable, almost damp, reminding me of crawling through the rocks at Mammoth Cave as a kid.

It was one of the most distinct and intimidating picture frames of my childhood.

I don't remember the exact words Pastor and I exchanged, but he was asking me what I thought about Jesus, if I knew he died on the cross for my sins. I believed, in a very elementary way, that Jesus had died for me and that he loved me, but still, I was frozen with fear, paralyzed right there in that cold metal chair. All I could think about was running back up those stairs to the warmth of the sunshine and the gravel and the fruit punch with the speed of a bounding kangaroo. I realize now that the tension in my spirit had nothing to do with the pastor and everything to do with the discomfort one experiences the first time they're confronted with Jesus.

This was around the same age that I started having the recurring nightmare of my childhood, instigated by the 1972 end-times film *A Thief in the Night*. A friend of our family had invited us to view it at their church, a noble, albeit failed, attempt at evangelism. In the opening scene, young Patty Jo wakes to find her husband's electric razor still buzzing but abandoned in their bathroom sink, her first sign that he, along with millions of others, had vanished in a premillennial rapture. (I still resent the way this frame, nearly thirty years later, is so cruelly singed in my mind.) Patty Jo, on the other hand, wasn't so lucky. She had been one of the unfortunate few who'd been left behind, Kirk Cameron style.

The setting of my dream often changed, but the result was always the same. The time I am thinking of now, and the one I remember most, takes place in a school. I am frantic, running up and down empty halls, panic frozen in my throat as I try to scream for help, the sound of my shoes slapping at the linoleum floors and echoing off the lockers; I am desperate to find one other person—*anyone*—hiding under a desk or in the janitor's closet or a bathroom stall, but to no avail. I run out to the parking lot only to find it abandoned as well, car doors opened and purses hastily strewn across the pavement. Horror sets in as I beg Jesus to tell me it's not true. I beg him to take me like he's taken the others, to tell me I'm not the only who is left to fend for her own eternity.

I awake abruptly and can't shake the terror that's wriggled into my bones. I finally muster the courage to get out of my bed, dodging the piles of clothes (i.e., monster arms) on my floor and dash into my parents' room where, as I often did after a bad dream, I wedge myself into the coveted middle spot and wait. Wait for my breathing to match the evenness of theirs, wait for the warmth of their bodies to lull me back to sleep, wait for the distressing images to fade into the night. Wait for peace. Wait for assurance. Wait for morning. Only the calming warmth of their bodies can't penetrate the affliction that's tape-wormed its way into my heart. I stare wide-eyed at the ceiling. I need somehow to change the dream, to convince Jesus of my devotion. And so I start to whisper, inaudibly at first: *I love you, Jesus. I love you, Jesus. I love you, Jesus.* I do this for a while.

But the more I repeat it, the more desperate I become, and my voice grows in pace with my conviction. *I love you, Jesus. I LOVE YOU, JESUS. I LOVE YOU, JESUS.* For I'm convinced, in the dark of that night, that my eternity rests on whether or not he can hear my voice.

Somewhere in the midst of that infinite dawn, my dad rolled over, kissed me wet on the forehead, and whispered back: *he loves you too.* I was asleep in an instant. The dream never taunted me again.

"What we believe about God," says A. W. Tozer, "is the most important thing about us."

Another frame came much later, this time as an adult while I was in Africa, my second trip in less than five years.

The first was with my friend Ruthanne who'd asked me to travel to Ethiopia with her to adopt her second child, Daniel Bereket Mintesnot, which means "What can't God do." At the time she'd asked me to go, we only knew one another from a distance, making it nothing short of a miracle that we'd both agreed. Weary and exhausted after nearly twenty-four hours of travel, we stood in customs at the Addis Ababa airport as a thunderstorm raged severe in the night.

We waited in line, too tired to speak, until I looked up from my suitcase, an incredulous smile suddenly playing on my lips, the irony of the moment settling in. "I can't believe you asked me to come to Africa with you," I said.

Without missing a beat (Ruthanne never misses a beat), she looked me square in the eyes. "I can't believe you came."

We both laughed.

The second time I was in Africa I traveled to Uganda with the nonprofit I'd eventually come to work for and became stuck in a gargantuan traffic jam in Kampala, the capital city. Unless you've actually experienced a Third World traffic jam, I'm afraid I have little to offer by way of description: hundreds (thousands?) of cars slanted at various angles with no clear traffic lanes; boda-bodas stacked three and four deep as their drivers try to thread themselves between vehicles; mounds of people swarming like schools of fish in every direction (night life is festive to say the least); donkeys, cows, and goats walking freely about, dogs scavenging for food; slabs of raw meat hanging from the tiny, tin-roofed shops squeezing the edges of the road; music blaring, horns beeping—a cacophony of noise and activity all swirling together that would compete with . . . honestly, I have no category. Nothing else I can even think of.

It was less than two hours before our flight and we were completely gridlocked, the kind of gridlocked where people turn off their ignitions, get out of their cars, and talk to drivers around them like they were tossing bags at a tailgate party. We'd already been in the car for six hours (on a trip that was supposed to take five) and hadn't seen a bathroom in seven. We were getting a little punchy.

I sat next to my friend Angie in the back of the seven-passenger van that we'd been traveling in for the last week; my friend Denise in the seat in front of us, all of us driven by the generous pastor and his wife, their four-year-old daughter Emma Grace asleep at our feet. Twenty-four hours before, sitting in the same seats we sat in now, we had thrown back a handful of fried grasshoppers we bought from a street vendor, an African delicacy, and laughed as hard as I've ever laughed in my whole life. But no one was laughing now. The imminence of missing our flight was looming; we were tired and ready to go home.

When it became clear that the traffic wasn't going to relent, Denise turned from the seat in front of me and said aloud what no one up to that point wanted to admit, "Um, yeah. There's no way we're making this flight." Although I couldn't see Angie's face, I could feel the panic emanating from her shoulders. In one swift move, she pulled her journal from her backpack and began scribbling with the urgency of a woman penning her last words.

I knew what she was doing. *Pray all you want. There's no way we're making this flight.* I might have rolled my eyes.

What happened next was for me no less shocking than the story of the woman at church who'd grabbed me a few weeks before and told me she'd been cured from stage four lung cancer with "no explanation," or reading the recent news report of the baby pulled alive from the Nepal earthquake after being buried four days. I might as well have seen Lazarus himself being raised from the dead, because all of a sudden, like a rainstorm commencing on a cloudless day, the traffic began to move. Drivers darted back inside their cars. Bodas bobbed and weaved. The meat and the music disappeared behind us, and not once did we stop again, not all the way to the airport.

A few days later, safely back on Western ground, Angie, Denise, and I were recounting the story, laughing at our idiosyncrasies and the fact that while Angie was facing the horror of missing our flight, Denise was trying to concoct a way to use the two-liter resting at her feet as her own private toilet. But then things turned a bit more serious, and I confessed the impact of the traffic jam, starting with my unbelief.

"Five days ago, I stood in a tin shack the size of a closet and watched as a fifteen-year-old girl laid her newborn twins on a filthy, ashen mattress atop a dirt floor. Odds are fair she'd been raped and left to fend for herself with no hope of providing for her children," I said. "I watched children parade around the mud walls of a school with no shoes, no chairs or desks, no school supplies. I listened to the despair of their teachers who were paid so little that sometimes they didn't have enough to eat. We sat in churches made of nothing more than plastic and sticks. The smell of poverty is still thick in my sinuses. I was pretty sure God didn't care whether or not we made our flight."

They listened quietly as we scraped pieces of food around our plates.

Angie was the first to speak. "I get it. You're right. We saw some pretty horrific things." She paused, thinking for a moment. "But that's the thing. What if God is big enough to care about all of it?"

I wasn't catching on. "What do you mean?" I said.

"What if he cares about the poverty in Africa *and* the kids in the school *and* the woman in the shack *and* whether or not we make our flight? What if he's big enough to care about all of it?"

I felt like the traffic was clearing all over again.

What we believe about God is the most important thing about us.

"I think I'm having a spiritual awakening," I said.

It's a picture frame in spiritual time. What does it look like to believe in a God who is big enough to care about the poverty of abused women and shoeless school children in Africa and babies pulled from earthquakes and friends being eaten away by cancer and all the millions of social injustices in our world . . . and a God who (simultaneously, nonetheless) holds our hands in the midst of all our kickball games and cold metal chairs and nightmares and traffic jams, our fears and doubts and insecurities, our wallowing in despair about the Stirring? A God who cares as equally and as passionately about the world as he does the way we offer ourselves to it? A God who cares about the way we follow him and serve his kingdom and the way we steward the dreams he's placed in our hearts, the calling he's given to each of us, big and small?

This is why it matters what we believe about God. If we believe God to be only powerful, we believe he'll bully his way into our dreams and force us one direction or the other. If we believe God to be only truth, we'll believe his chief concern is the number of hours we've logged and the results of our performance. If we believe God to be only distant Creator, we'll believe he's just sitting back, watching our call unfold in an armchair in heaven, in between bites of Buffalo wings and TV timeouts. If we believe God to be only concerned about our personal calling, we'll believe he wants us to pursue it apart from what he's already doing in a world that needs us as much as it doesn't. If we believe God only ever cares about what we want to do when we grow up, we'll forget that his primary purpose for us lies in the person we choose to become. We'll simply assume, as Miroslav Volf says, that who we believe God to be and who God truly is are one and the same.

If we believe the wrong things about God, we may end up believing that he's sitting across from us, arms folded, as we squirm in a cold, metal chair waiting to know what we think of him, or that he's the guy stretched out in a big white Cadillac flashing his crown of glory while we work our butts off trying to scrape together a good life for our family, doing the best we can. Rather than being a Father who cares intimately about what's inside us, the sustainer and inspirer of our dreams, he becomes at worst a disdainful enemy, at best a distant cheerleader.

But none of these things are true about the good and perfect character of God.

One Sunday morning, somewhere along the way, a missionary grabbed me by the arm after I had finished teaching a class, a weathered old man who'd spent the better part of his life in a developing country and whom I'd never met before. Out of context for the moment, he felt compelled to tell me that we so often think God is calling us to the next great thing that we forget that he's calling us first and foremost to himself. Not a new idea in the theology of time, but new to me. We serve a God who calls us first and foremost to himself, a God who steps into earth with his calloused hands and dirty feet and asks us to follow him.

About six months later, not long after I sat across from Pastor Stern in the cold metal chair, I got the lead in the church's Christmas cantata. At the end of the play, the audience was gracious with their affection toward us. Showered with the adoration of a standing ovation, suddenly and without warning, I felt the uncomfortable tension in my spirit again and had the uncontrollable urge to run. While all the other children were soaking it in, I slipped, as quickly as I could, to the back of the stage, down the red velvet stairs into the cold basement, and stood outside the room where Pastor Stern had first asked me about Jesus.

I have often looked back and described that as my salvation moment, but now I'm not sure that's true. I don't remember praying a prayer or "asking Jesus into my heart"; I just remember the way my chest felt like it was collapsing in on itself, how certain I was that none other than the imperial weight of glory itself was enfolding me, wrapping me in the totality of its indescribable holiness, a nameless feeling, and how at the tender age of nine all I could do was slide my body along the dampness of the wall, to slump in the corner and weep, for the Spirit of God had fallen upon me.

It wouldn't be the last time I'd experience the pressing sacredness of such a moment, and over the years of offering myself to God and encountering his grace, I've learned to trust these frames for what they are—the presence of a God who calls us to himself, who wants us to know in the midst of all our fears and doubts and insecurities about what we're supposed to do with our lives, that he is with us and for us and more than big enough for all of it. He quiets our deepest fears. He calms the depths of our longing. I've learned to stop questioning whether the Stirring is true or not, if it makes sense, to stop doubting if it was God or if it was me or if I made it up, and instead embrace it, listen to it, and welcome it when it presses in.

What we believe about God is the most important thing about us.

And in welcoming it, I believe what it's saying, what it's calling me to, what it says to me about my life, my future, about who he is, is true. Because I believe that the God who is big enough to hang the stars in the sky, to raise the dead to life, to bring about the biggest revolution in human history, to make blind men see and lame men walk, to bind the brokenhearted and set the captives free—and to clear the traffic in Africa—also chose that moment in the basement of that church to reveal himself to an insignificant young girl who he was madly in love with.

He's always big enough.

Years later, as an adult, when I was trying to first pen this story, I mentioned the pastor to my friend. She was confused. Remember, your pastor when we were kids, I said. Pastor Stern? She laughed; Pastor Stout you mean?

Turns out his name wasn't Stern at all.

7

Courage

The thief comes only to steal and kill and destroy; I have come that they may have life, and have it to the full.

JESUS (JOHN 10:10)

have bizarre dreams when I'm discouraged about the Stirring. This time I had a dream about a snake.

I am standing in a brown and cloudy river, heat stuffed so deep in my throat that I struggle to breathe. The Amazon, if I had to guess, is where I'd say I am, albeit, perhaps, a naive Midwestern version. The banks of the river slope steep into lush green, and would feel claustrophobic if not for the large mouth of the river opening wide at one end. A group of people gather under a canopy of looming trees, ankle deep in the muddy water, and listen as a rugged tour guide speaks eloquently about their surroundings. I am separate from them, far, but I can hear what the guide is saying. He is telling everyone about the snakes.

Dangerous, predatory, poisonous—one ounce of venom means certain death. It is then that I feel it, a small movement, a gentle swirl of water—the rush of fear cementing my feet into the mud of the river, paralyzing me in the depths of the quicksand as I catch the subtle flick of the snake's rearing head. When it strikes me, the pain is searing and hot, the thick of my lower leg burns like it's been imprinted by a branding iron, then gives way to nausea. It's a weird feeling to know you're going to die, even if it's only a dream.

I am somehow transported, like one magically is in dreams, to the dim lights of a hospital. Writhing turns calm as the intensity of the pain begins to dull. Death was inevitable, they said, but the bite has somehow not killed me. I am, in fact, still alive. I survived the thing that I had most feared; I have been spared. The fear that paralyzed me didn't kill me.

When I awoke, I could still feel the searing heat on my ankle; I carried it with me the whole of that next day in the same way I carried these words, like a shawl over my bare shoulders, "The thief comes only to steal and kill and destroy. I came that they may have life and have it abundantly" (John 10:10 ESV).

I believe God sometimes chooses to speak to us through our dreams. Whether this was that or not, I guess I can't be certain, but the message was received, and I chose to believe it. Fear not, the Scriptures say, for he is with you, even to the ends of the age.

His feet hit hard, uneven, loud. The gangly rhythm reminded me of the sound a flat tire makes on the highway, one awkward thump followed by flopping rubber. One side of his face sloped toward the tip of his shoulder; one arm dangled lifelessly by his side. I assumed it was a stroke but had no intention of asking, so instead, I forced myself to politely look away, focusing on my own tired workout, at the rusted dumbbells that lay at my toes. But the sound kept drawing me back. *Thump, flop, slide. Thump, flop, flop.* Emotion welled in the back of my throat, and one thought pushed all others out of my mind: *Courage. This is the most courageous thing I've ever seen.* Courage whose only witnesses would be me and a handful of sweaty vagabonds scattered throughout the armpit basement of an old YMCA.

If only all of us could be so brave.

When we first had kids and were still living in Ohio, I coached a high school volleyball team with my friend Lisa. We decided (actually she decided) to kick off our season with the ultimate team-building event: a high ropes course. I say she, because I never would have imposed such absurdity on myself. I'm terrified of heights. I often imagine what it would be like to tumble over the Adams Street bridge into the Chicago River on a cold January day, or plummet off the edge of a mountain during a hike, or for my children to plunge headlong over the ill-equipped railings on a vacation to Niagara Falls. The list goes on and on.

This morning, however, I stood with the girls on a soft bed of woodchips, a green canopy sheltering us from the first signs of the sun, tugging at my harness, fiddling with my chinstrap, the instructor's final safety reminders ticking the edges of my ears. A contraption of obstacles hung high in the sky above our heads, which I pretended, for the sake of the team, were no big thing. Then my eyes came to rest on the highest point of the course: one fat log, an eternity long, floating above all the others and a faint nausea threatened my breakfast.

Not that one, I said. Partly a promise to myself, partly a plea to the mercy of God. Courage apparently has its bounds. *I'll do anything but that one.*

A few hours later, I found myself standing on a two-by-two platform a thousand feet in the air (that's how high it feels when you're the one looking down instead of up), staring at the exact log on which I declared I would never brush a toe. A thirty-foot tightrope lay between me and the other side and was my only face-saving way of getting down. I pushed out a shaky breath and closed my eyes. *How did I get here?*

"Coach!" A voice zipping through the wind.

Whitney, a sophomore with the curious eyes of fawn whom I adored, sat on the platform across from me, legs dangling, carefree, to their death. My façade was clearly waning.

"Coach! You can do this. Just don't look down," she said. "Look at me, Coach, right here in the eye. Just look at me and make your way across. One step at a time."

Then and there, I made a bold and conscious decision: I chose to listen to her voice. I chose to actually believe that what she was saying was true. I locked my eyes on hers, pushed all of the air out of my lungs, and with one bashful step, abandoned the shifting safety of my platform.

"Eyes right here, Coach. You got this."

And then in a most surprising and charitable gesture, Whitney, a girl whose faith was undisclosed to me, began to sing into the whites of my eyes: *"Jesus loves me, this I know. For the Bible tells me so.* Don't look down, Coach. Look right here at me. *Little ones to him belong, they are weak but he is strong."* She sang it to me sweetly, gently, reassuringly, repeatedly, until I made my way to the other side. I didn't take my eyes off her, not one time, until my feet rested, weary from their journey, solidly on the other side.

Fear is an emotion I'd rather have consumed by the gas of the atmosphere. Like the dead of winter, like rush-hour traffic, like mosquitos, I often don't understand its reason for existing. Fear is pungent, unremorseful, preying on the most vulnerable cubicles inside of us that hold that which we most love, that which we most desire. Fear digs its talons into us, laying open shards of flesh and skin, leaving the scars vulnerable to whatever fables its cunning tongue wants to spin. It tells us that we're better off never trying, to save ourselves the embarrassment of failure and rejection and of others laughing at us, to wrap ourselves inside our cocoons, to isolate, sneering that we're better off alone. Except when we're alone, we're easier to pick off. Fear is the impetus behind all of our "not that ones."

Courage, on the other hand, "is not the absence of fear," Nelson Mandela says, "but triumph over it. The brave man is not he who does not feel afraid, but he who conquers that fear." *Conquer* is a strong word, but when it comes to our dreams, it becomes imperative to choose courage in spite of our fear. We must not let fear paralyze us, not let it snatch our hope, because when we call its bluff, it can actually propel us to action. It allows us to posture ourselves in a way that perhaps we otherwise would not, and that's usually how dreams find their first awkward step. We therefore must take a hold of courage, stuff it inside of us, even if we're reluctant at first, until it permeates every pore of our humanity, and then let it leak, stealthly, until it finally overtakes the fear.

"You gain strength, courage and confidence by every experience in which you really stop to look fear in the face," said Eleanor Roosevelt in her book *You Learn by Living.* "You are able to say to yourself, 'I have lived through this horror. I can take the next thing that comes along.' You must do the thing you think you cannot do." Or has Meg Cabot says in the *Princess Diaries,* "The brave may not live forever, but the cautious do not live at all."

At some point we will inevitably begin to ask what our dreams will cost us, if they are worth the sacrifice of letting go of our fear. For the more secure we feel, the more we have to be afraid of losing. Sometimes our biggest dreams induce our biggest fears. We work through all the "am I good enough?" "can I do it?" "does anyone like me?" stuff, but then we're forced into the reality that, if we choose to pursue them, our dreams may actually affect our lives, they may actually cost us something, and we may have to sacrifice things that are important to us in order to accomplish them, and we curl back under the fear. Without courage, we let the thief have his way with us. I wonder how often have I failed, not because I actually failed but because I didn't have the courage to try.

And so, despite our fear, we have to take a step of faith, offering ourselves to God, to others, to our dreams and to the world when we have no idea what it will cost us or what the outcome will be; we don't actually know what the price tag will be until we are finally standing at the register and the mousy cashier with the dirty brown hair scans the items, and for a moment we wonder if she's ever going to stop because we didn't realize how many items we actually laid down. And then the final price comes up on the screen, and we realize we don't actually have that much money in our pockets. We don't actually have that much money in all the world. We dig frantically through every nook and cranny of every pocket, and no matter what, we can't come up with enough. So instead we scrape together what we have, the pennies and dimes so caked in grit and rust that we can barely pull them apart (you think about cleaning them but you know it's futile and you're too weary too care) and the one stray quarter all covered in the snotty lint of an old Kleenex, and you open your fingers and hold your palm flat before her, hoping she'll see the sorry and desperate look on your face, the shame washing over you, and take pity on you. And so you hold it there, standing in a puddle of humiliation, as these words limp through your heart: *This is all I have. I know it's not enough, but this is all I have.*

And to your astonishment, moved by your meager display of courage, she takes it. All of it. Even the rust and the lint and the grit, and she plunks it into the register. She puts your items in a bag, silently, one by one. Then she catches your eye, offers the kind of gentle smile that only comes with knowing, and you smile weakly back at her, the shame lifting just a speck, and you turn toward the door. She took all that you had to offer and sent you into the world.

And you become more of who you were meant to be.

Without courage, when we insist on mandating to God which things we will or will not do, we never even make our way to the register; we never step off the platform. We never empty our pockets and offer ourselves to someone else, to see if they'll take what we have even when we know it's not enough. Not only not enough, but messy and dirty and covered in lint and snot.

Challenge by choice, the ropes master told us. You will challenge yourself by your own choice, not because anyone else is pressuring you to do so. Courage has to come from within, from believing in ourselves, believing in God. It takes courage to offer ourselves to the Stirring, which in and of itself is a scary thing, but maybe sometimes courage is easier than we think if we just make the choice to put it on display.

I think back to the guy on the YMCA track, thumping and flopping along, not afraid of what others may think or what he looks like, if he'll fail or what it will cost him. He simply plods along, and when he's done, wipes the sweat from his brow, the same as the rest of us, and goes on about his day.

.8

Choices

*But there are moments when one has to choose
between living one's own life, fully, entirely, completely—
or dragging out some false, shallow, degrading existence
that the world in its hypocrisy demands.*

OSCAR WILDE, *LADY WINDEMERE'S FAN*

After the Stirring, I didn't really have any intention of going back to work. Well before becoming a parent, I imagined a life spent baking fresh cookies in a spotless house with a never-fading smile plastered to my always-pleasant face, but it didn't take long for reality to set in. Raising young children was hard, and I wasn't terribly good at it. So when Sadie and Clay got into school full time and my days opened up, I dove into a dream to speak and write with vigor, saying yes to every opportunity that came my way. No invitation was too big or too small (and mostly all of them were small). I felt like I was coming alive, hitting my stride. Doors began to open. I was stepping into my dream. I was doing what I wanted to do along my way to becoming who I wanted to be.

I began teaching regularly at several large communities in my church. I published my first article in a real magazine that paid me eighty-seven dollars. I won a scholarship for an essay I had written for a writer's conference. I started blogging. I preached a few sermons. I got invitations to speak in other communities, led a couple retreats, and managed a blog for a bestselling author. I helped found a writers' collective that quickly grew, drawing writers from across the country and turning the heads of publishing industry professionals. I visited a few colleges to look into pursuing a master's degree in theology and communication. I joined the PTA. I coached my kids' basketball team.

The only thing I wasn't doing, besides the occasional check here and there, was getting paid.

Since relocating to Chicago, the realization of living in one of the most affluent counties in the country on a one-income pastor's salary was increasingly taking its toll. The stress of trying to make ends meet was palpable and seemed to be getting more difficult by the month. Our sixty-year-old house needed windows and a roof and a water heater and a bathroom free from mold, and the kids were only getting more expensive by the minute.

When I was sitting on my bed flipping through a book one morning, Eric gently approached me as he got ready for work. We'd had endless conversations about the Stirring. He was supportive, but also a realist. I could tell he wasn't sure how to say what he was about to say, a cat precipitously approaching its prey.

"So I'm glad you're, like, living out your dream and all that, and I'm really glad God is speaking to you. It's fun to see you so passionate about what you're doing, but if you're going to spend all your time volunteering for stuff . . . um . . . do you think you could . . . uh . . . maybe do something where you get paid?"

Reality bites. We needed the money. Practicality took precedence over my dreams. Knowledge, credibility, esteem, and a brain doused with ideas and creativity and potential would have to wait to be unleashed on another day.

I put out a couple of feelers, but after being an at-home mom for eight years, no one much cared that I could teach a few classes or had started a blog that few people would ever read. My résumé had some gaping holes. And then there was logistics, the small fact that we were raising two children with no family members within five hundred miles. At some point along the way, I came across an editorial internship at a local publishing house that I thought could be a good fit. I could do a ten-week internship and work around the kids' schedules.

"So, let me get this straight," Eric said. "You're going to go back to work and still not get paid?"

"Well . . . yeah, but . . ." By this point I actually thought it was a brilliant idea.

"Doesn't that kind of defeat the purpose?" he said.

"Well kind of. Maybe. But not really," I said. "It's just for a little while. Maybe it will turn into something. You'll see."

In November I scheduled an interview with an editor. We hit it off immediately. He asked good questions, listened well, and was particularly funny. I remember thinking how impressive my writing career had been to that point and how certain I was that he'd be impressed too. At the end of our time, he caught me off guard by asking when I wanted to start.

"Um, oh . . . okay, sure," I said. Some decisions are made before you actually know that you're going to make them. I was thirty-five years old and about to accept an unpaid internship. "How about sometime in the spring?"

Despite the fact that on my first day someone asked me "what year I was," the internship was a blast. I loved the stimulation of being back in the flow of a work environment and was fascinated by the publishing process. I was inspired by the atmosphere of ideas and words and was geeked out by people who loved talking about books as much as I did. The editor and I became fast friends.

Somewhere along the way we started talking about my writing, and he asked me what I wanted to write about. I've learned that some people want to write because they feel like they have something to say, something the world needs to know before it can take its next breath. For me, it's the opposite. I write because I enjoy the creative process; I'm intrigued and challenged by creating something from scratch, laboring over all of its intricacies and complexities until something captivating rises out of the ashes, a story worth commemorating, a memory worth encapsulating, a heritage worth preserving and passing on. I write because I want people to feel something, not so much (or at all) because I have something to say that I think they should *know*. All this to say, I break into an anxious sweat when someone asks me as daunting and as pointed of a question as what I want to write about.

"Dreams, I think," I said. "I'm passionate about people living out their dreams."

"Hmmm. Dreams are good," he said, shifting his eyebrows back and forth, one high, one low and then vice versa. "Dreams are always good."

Later I'd come to learn that this was one of the qualities about him that I'd particularly come to admire. The eyebrows, yes, but as an editor, he understood the gravitas of possessing the fragile responsibility of holding someone's dreams, a sand dollar whose fate lay solely in the encumbrance of his grip, and had learned the kind and delicate art of not crushing aspirations outright.

At the end of my internship, an executive came to my "office," which, in reality, was a small desk tucked away in the library. He told me his assistant was leaving and that he was looking to hire someone in the fall. He wondered if I might be interested.

I am the least administrative person I know.

"Sure, I'd love to talk more," I said.

A few weeks later, a woman called for what I was told would be to schedule the interview. Not wanting to miss her call, I picked up the phone on my way out to pick up the kids from school. I parked in my normal pick-up spot and listened intently. After a couple of minutes, the horror of what was happening began to settle in. She wasn't calling to *schedule* the interview. This *was* the interview. I spotted Sadie and Clay running across the playground toward the van, backpacks flopping wildly on their small frames, and I quickly locked the doors. For forty-five minutes, I pulled the car back and forth along the curb while my kids banged on the windows, screaming at me to let them in, me snapping violently through the tinted glass, floundering over every question she asked.

It was an awful interview (a fact to which she would later agree). Miraculously I got a second interview, which led to a third interview and culminated with a job offer. I accepted, somehow landing myself a job that I'm not sure I actually wanted.

"Maybe it is because the great decisions are not made at some particular moment in time, but deep within us have been so long in the making," Frederick Beuchner writes, "that we find ourselves acting on them before we are altogether conscious of having decided to."

I don't know if that's actually true in this case, but I'd like to believe it was a necessary step as I kept trying to find my way.

9

Voices

*I have thought about the people I have known
and the things that have happened that have, for
better or worse, left the deepest mark on me.*

FREDERICK BUECHNER, *THE SACRED JOURNEY*

I am about ten years old. I am in the living room with my
brother David and his best friend Michael. It was always either
our house or theirs; the three of us left to play while our moms
sat at the kitchen table playing an endless game of Rummy or
Backgammon, swigging Pepsi from glass bottles while a cloud of
cigarette smoke hung heavy over their heads. My companions are
only a year older than me, but they exploit their self-imposed
superiority at every opportunity. On this occasion, for a reason
that only now seems out of place, they are discussing *To Kill a
Mockingbird*. I hear the title and I sneer. *Stupid boys.* Finally the
tables have turned, and for the first time in our adolescent relationship I am sure that I have the upper hand.

I embrace the fullness of the sarcasm percolating in my voice,
"Yeah . . . *that* sounds like a good book."

The laughing was gut level and mean, a crooked finger confirming the insecurities that, at least for this one moment in time, I was certain were false. I don't remember an explanation of the profundity of the book or why it earned Harper Lee the 1961 Pulitzer Prize.

I only remember the laughing.

Sometimes I wonder if there is a quiet space left in the world, the kind of quiet that comes with stillness, silence that fills and surrounds and creates space to think, to imagine, to dream. Space so completely free from distraction that one can actually see the silence as it rises out of the ground, a nebula crawling out of the earth, gaining volume as it finally billows into a dense cloud, suspended over top of us, lingering, until we feel it descending, protective and warm, an x-ray blanket coming to rest on our shoulders, covering us so heavily and securely that we're content in its peaceful void.

I'm reminded of this as I sit in a congested coffee shop on this Saturday morning, incapable of stringing two conspicuous thoughts together. My eyes pan the tables, and I can't help but wonder if silence has ever existed throughout the equator of time, even back when the earth was formless and empty, when darkness was over the surface of the deep and the Spirit of God hovered over the waters (Genesis 1:2).

I've craved that kind of silence, the silence the waters knew, both in the midst of the everyday and in the darkest and most desperate times I have known, but I've always found myself left wanting.

The espresso machine grinds and whirs, breaking my thoughts, and I almost hurl my latte in its direction, because what the flurry pushes me to is not silence but more noise, for noise begets noise. I pick up my phone, check my email and my Facebook feed, Google the GE repair site to figure out why the sensor in my washing machine has stopped working. Anything but to be present where I am right now, trying to think and to concentrate, to be attentive to my dreams.

This is my long way of getting to the point: the problem with all of this noise is that it clouds out the voices we often most need to hear. Voices that our souls need as desperately as we need the quiet; voices that cut through the noise, over the grind and whir of the espresso machine, both past and present, and remind us of the things we most need reminded of: the very best parts of who we are. And who we are not.

Some voices don't look us in the soul or the eye or even in the general vicinity of our face, but instead look at the hairs that brush the tops of our head, the gray crown of our skull; they are shifty, antsy, looking right past us to the rest of the room for something more enticing that will captivate their attention. And because they don't really see us, their words follow the same path as their eyes; they skip off the top of our heads and fall lifelessly to the remnants of dirt and grime and spilled alcohol that coagulate on the floor. These voices are so self-absorbed and overcome with apathy that the only sound they hear is the blood coursing through their own veins. These voices aren't worth our time or disappointment. They are, in fact, benign. Other voices perforate our dreams; slit them so sharply with disbelief that we're left reeling with insolence and shock. They see us, but they injure us.

I don't know which are worse: the candor of the ones who directly tell us we can't achieve or the ones who listen to our dreams, who actually see us, and then dismiss us entirely.

But still, some voices take us by the hand, stare purposefully and intently into the whites of our eyes. They speak to both the passion and the fear that live inside of us and they say that which is true, that which speaks the very essence of us into being. They make our frames stand taller, our hearts softer, turn our eyes to God. They make our vision clearer. They are truth and beauty and grace. They call us to something more than just what is inside of our own small selves. They make us look inward in a way that pushes our gaze outward to others and the needs of the world.

They ascend the hovering noise and they overcome it, and in turn, we begin to overcome it too, so that certain melodies become distinct while others fade away. They encourage and inspire us to step out and to believe that we, too, can rise above the noise, that we aren't just adding more static to this world, but creating a symphony that's worthy to be played.

My freshman year at Ohio University, a group of girlfriends and I threw a party for our friend who wasn't returning the following year. We had spent the last nine months in what my parents called "a year-long slumber party," the kind of cumulative quality time that led us to plan weekend getaways long after we graduated and eventually stand in one another's weddings. In 1994, with the exception of the mix tape, no gift communicated the depths of love and friendship better than a picture collage, and we had worked hard to get it just right for our friend, complete with funny phrases taped above our faces, capturing the essence of who we were. Sitting knee to knee on the dorm room floor, I couldn't wait for her to unveil the gift. When she did, along with everyone else, I laughed long and hard—until I noticed something that wasn't there before. My laughter halted, an abrupt stop, and I found myself sinking in a puddle of betrayal, bewildered to find that one of my roommates had pasted a picture of the earth revolving around my head: evidently, the essence of me. I left the room in haste and spent the next hour hiding in the bathroom—but I'd spend the next twenty years determined not to become the person she caricatured me to be. It was a roast-like gesture that my soul never overcame.

During the years, I've tried to drown out that voice, shake it off as inconsequential, as one that was so far outside of my essence that its only reason for existing was absurdity. But flecks of shame stay with me to this day, the looming globe poking me, taunting me, clanging in the back of my mind each time I forget someone's name, each time I dominate a conversation, each time I interrupt, each time I utter the words "I've been meaning to call you . . . ," each time I spend so much time feeling sorry for myself when a friend misses a significant moment in my life that I forget that during the same time she's had a few of her own.

My pastor, Dan, gave a sermon in which he said the worst thing inside of us—worse than all the negative voices and the wounds they inflict—is our own fear that what they say may actually be true. And so what we most need in our lives is voices who will speak to the fear—the fear that we're not enough or that we never will be enough, not good enough or smart enough or capable enough or whatever enough—and draw courage out of us to speak the truth of who we are. They also need to be willing to tell us who we are not: for sometimes we need the sting of who we are not in order to fully accept and grow into who we actually are.

The gift of my roommate's voice was exactly that, a gift that would challenge my character and humbly push me toward the becoming. To be more holy, more interested in other people's lives than my own, to take seriously the responsibility of being a voice that doesn't skate off others but lands solidly in the core of their soul and helps them become too.

Not like all these distracting voices in this coffee shop, the rumbling, mumbling noises all around us that distract us to the point of lethargy, numbness, complete fragmentation and chaos and confusion, that drive us to more distraction. But the ones that hone in, laser in, give us moments of crystal clarity, the ones that we turn over and over again in our head, that won't leave us alone, that keep running through our minds long after the actual words have vaporized. Voices that call something out of us, something we never saw before, something we thought might be inside of us but never dared to tell anyone for fear of the laughter.

But they saw it in us first.

Maybe you are the only one who remembers their voice, maybe the person who spoke the words doesn't even remember saying them—but for you, they were hope. They were inspiration. They were courage and confidence and strength. They made you take one step further in a direction you never imagined yourself capable except for that one shard of encouragement, that one cascading pebble that connected with a remnant of yourself deep inside that you weren't sure anyone would ever see or know but that you've always known—despite all the noise—was the truest part of you.

We must grab hold of these voices (and we must persist if we are to grab hold of them), and believe in them as much as they believe in us, so that we can cut out all of the superfluous sounds that threaten to drown us each day. Then the noise will fade into the background and the only voices we will hear are the ones who matter, the ones who lead us into the next space of the becoming, the ones who teach us more about who we are and who we want to be until we walk in rhythm with them. For the other voices never knew the real us, the parts that are worthy to shine.

"Vocation does not come from a voice 'out there' calling me to become something I am not," Parker Palmer said. "It comes from a voice 'in here' calling me to be the person I was born to be, to fulfill the original selfhood given me at birth by God."

And in trusting that God himself speaks through the voices in order to call us up from dust, we begin to more clearly recognize the one voice that endures, a God who summons us no matter what we accomplish or how great we fail. A God who says we are loved, forgiven, restored, and redeemed. We are cherished through righteousness and protected by grace. We are safe and secure. We are flawed and broken. We are gifted and called. We are. And we are not.

For his is the voice that sustains us as we step into our dreams. His is the voice that calls us to step into the parts of ourselves that were just waiting, even before we knew they were waiting, for someone to give us a name.

10

Naming

*I believe in the power and mystery of naming things.
Language has the capacity to transform our cells, rearrange
our learned patterns of behavior and redirect our thinking.
I believe in naming what's right in front of us
because that is often what is most invisible.*

EVE ENSLER, *THE VAGINA MONOLOGUES*

I wonder if anyone told them.

It's the question that haunts me at every funeral I attend.

This time her name is Julia.

Her medical record was clean until, at the age of eleven, she was blindsided by mitochondrial disease, a horrible and rare and fatal disease, a sadistic thief that stole her adolescence by chipping away at her sight, her hearing, her nervous system, and her gross motor skills until it finally stole her last breath at the age of twenty. I actually didn't know Julia; I became a friend of her dad's well after the illness left her mostly homebound, but I was touched by her eloquence, a spirit, everyone said, that couldn't be deterred, even as the disease feasted on her cells. Her death is the kind of senseless tragedy that makes one question the goodness of God, the cruelty and harshness of life, and ask what parts of themselves would ever recover had they to endure the same fate. *Diagnosed at age eleven.* The same age as Clay as I sat at her funeral. I shivered under the steeple of the sanctuary.

Her mother read her eulogy, saying she was the type of person who always had the courage to follow her dreams. Her sister melted, racked with sobs. Her father embraced them both as they walked off the stage. There wasn't a dry eye in the house. Watching another be swallowed by grief is a harrowing experience, no matter how close you are to the pain. Compassion is universal when it involves the loss of a child.

As I listened to others speak of Julia, my eyes spanned the room. I found myself wondering if the lives of the people sitting in these wooden pews were intimately touched by this beautiful life or if they were more of a bystander like me. I wonder if they knew the kind of person she was. And I found myself thinking it again.

I wonder if anyone told her.

The party almost didn't happen.

For the better part of her twelfth year, I had a dream of throwing Sadie a coming-of-age party. For years I'd been railing on the fact that, as a culture, we don't have a formal rite of passage at any age, but the true inkling for the party began with a conversation with Pastor Dan over salmon and mimosas at a crowded Easter brunch, me commenting on how Sadie was drawn to strong, independent women, him asking if I knew why. Me staring blankly back at him (mostly because I was confounded that I'd never thought to ask) and him coming to my rescue, spitting out the words with unapologetic certitude: "She's drawn to them because she's one of them. She recognizes her own kind."

That's what gave me the idea for the party.

I waited until after her birthday, three days after Christmas, and then I waited another week. I dragged my feet for fear of being the part of me that I most was, the part that has a tendency to annoy people most: sappy, sentimental, overly reflective. I drafted the invitation, rewrote it, and hit save a thousand times. I closed my computer. We weren't eulogizing her. She wasn't getting married; she wasn't christening her first child. She was simply turning thirteen. *This was a stupid idea.* But then the rolodex of images flooded my mind, a family mourning the loss of their daughter at an unfathomable age, and the words skated through my mind again. *I wonder if anyone told her.* I hit send.

Knowing what I know now, had I not gone through with the party—a becoming party, I had called it—the regret would have swallowed me whole. The evening was one of the most beautiful I've ever known.

Sadie lay slumped in an oversized bean bag, acting every minute of her thirteen years, but I knew her well enough to know it was her way of managing her own awkwardness about receiving the gift that was to come. About twenty women were gathered who had been part of her young life; they were the strong women to which she was drawn that I had told Dan about. I had given them two simple instructions: share one word of affirmation and one word of advice. I sat in a nearby chair and gently commenced the evening, looking each person in the eye, explaining the difference they made, known or unaware, by simply being who they were and offering it into the life of a child.

And then I yielded the floor.

I listened as one by one the women gathered in the room that night named my daughter. Words, so many words, poured forth. Words of encouragement: *Your smile lights up a room.* Words of affirmation: *You're a leader.* Words of advice: *Avoid girl drama and boys.*

Words of wisdom: *Whatever is pure, whatever is noble, whatever is lovely, think of such things.* Words of challenge: *Be kind in the midst of your leadership and seek out those who are on the fringes, for they too need a friend.* But most importantly words of truth.

Truth that washed over her, washed over me, washed over the decades represented by each person who sat in the room because that's what truth does. It's the quintessential nature of truth. It pierces. It washes. It cleanses. It settles over us and reminds us of that which is right and lovely and noble in one another and in this world at the same time it reminds us of all that is broken with both; it threads and binds us together by reminding us of that which is universally true. We spend much of life sharing the same fears, the same insecurities; we ask the same questions about who we are and where we fit in this world; we make the same mistakes, we long for the desires that fulfill our deepest needs. We wonder if anyone will sit with us at lunch or invite us to the dance or if we studied enough to pass the exam. We wonder if we will be found out. We want. We ache. We need.

We are people who possess and distort and so need the truth.

And we need to speak it into one another if we're ever to live out our dreams.

I wonder if anyone told her.

My sister-in-law Sharon lives on the Farm and couldn't come to the party. Instead, she sent this note:

Accept the woman who looks back at you from the mirror each morning. In the years to come, you'll love her, hate her, laugh with her, cry with her, rejoice with her, high-five her, ignore her, doubt her, yell at her and maybe wish she was someone else, but you need to learn to accept her for who she is with all of her strengths and all of her weaknesses. *You are fearfully and wonderfully made* say the Psalms and sometimes it's easy to believe that, but sometimes it's very, very hard. Before you can enter into a healthy relationship or friendship with anyone else, you need to first accept and later grow to love the woman who looks back at you. There is a quiet, strong sense of satisfaction and contentment that comes from accepting yourself exactly as God made you.

And truth names.

God named the days and the nights, the waters and the earth; God named Adam, Adam named Eve, and together they named the garden and all that was in it. And on and on it goes for the continuum of time.

There's a kind of naming that's easy, a simple combination of letters that allows us to identify something based on its characteristics, its chemical or physical make-up. Ball. Bridge. Rock. Chair. But when we exhume identity, actual personhood with all of its raw humanity and bind it to a name, it becomes an exquisite work of art whose brush strokes color and shape and form in a way that uniquely brings inanimate objects to life. Names that actually name a person are something to behold.

With the richness of the party draped still over my shoulders, I thought once again about how one of the great tragedies of our Western culture is that we have a nasty habit of waiting until we're standing at someone's funeral to speak the very truth about them that we saw all along, the truth that most made them who they are and the truth that, perhaps, they most needed to know if they were ever going to step into the person they were created to be.

I was in my thirties before anyone offered this gift to me.

The first time it happened I was sitting on a blue flowered and upholstered couch across from my friend Adele. I had just finished my first teaching assignment of significance and she wanted to "process how it went." Bracing myself for the worst, I was surprised when, instead of walloping me with critique, she took me by the hands and with tears in her eyes said, "Let me tell you what I see."

It happened again as I sat across from my friend Bill in a crowded Starbucks. "If you set out to write, I believe that you could." It happened as my friend Tracey reassured me, "I believe when you finally figure out what you want to say, it's going to be really great." It happened as I talked to my friend Amy under the hanging trees of a Little League park, "You have a depth in your spirit that is longing to come out." It happened when my friend Nancy, years ago, pulled me into her dining room and showed me the spot on her shelf she'd been saving for a book I never knew if I'd write. It happened when my friend Jeff told me I needed to quit my job. It happened as the words of Pastor Dan poured over me the first Wednesday of Lent, as he put the ashes on my forehead and told me I was dust and then I wept because the words he whispered in my ear next, I'm certain, were the very breath of God.

Naming is different from the voices that rise above the noise. Naming happens when someone has the courage to sit across a table from us, their life from ours, look us intently in the eye and name what they see. Naming is profound; it's an indescribable moment when the hands of time stop because someone has reached into our chest and pulled our hearts right out; they hold it in their hands (carefully, because they know one wrong word could crush it), and they whisper truth, not over it but into it, in a way that delivers a piece of who we are. Like a prophet shouting into the wilderness, it comes straight from God.

When I said thank you to a friend who did this very thing for me, he brushed it off, not because he didn't recognize the profundity of it, but because for him, it was the only natural thing to do. "I only said out loud what I saw in front of me," he said.

And while the words are meant for that specific space in time, for that part of who we are that needs to come alive in a singular moment, a child cowering in darkness being called into the light, they will stay with us forever and change who we are. We will go back to them again and again, in our darkest nights when we've lost hope about the Stirring and who we're trying to become, because they are the words that will remind us that who we are is visible to other people, that what we were made to do is seen, that God has uniquely gifted and wired us and that we didn't hear him wrong when he called us. They are the words that compel us to carry on with our dreams for just one more day.

We also must not be afraid to give this gift of naming away. It takes courage to step outside of ourselves and speak to the invisible, to breathe life into someone when at our core we feel like it may be snatching a piece of our own, like somehow it threatens our own name. But we must set this aside because it's a lie. In naming someone else, we actually become more of who we are. It strengthens our own character, our confidence, our fortitude. By giving a piece of ourselves away, we get something back.

To name someone is to make them known. And to know our own selves better.

I'm profoundly perplexed by the idea that, given his grandeur, his omnipotence and majesty, his eminence and glory, God chooses to call each of us by name. That he chooses to know us so uniquely and intently and completely, in such a way that he finds the right words to pierce our souls, to speak just to us, as gently and intimately as a mother rubbing noses with her adoring child. There may, perhaps, be no other phenomenon I find so perplexing and awesome than this about God.

He names us first.

He names us not only in our giftedness and calling and dreams, he names us first and foremost as his children. Beloved, redeemed, forgiven, called. "For you are a chosen people. You are royal priests, a holy nation, God's very own possession. As a result, you can show others the goodness of God, for he called you out of the darkness into his wonderful light" (1 Peter 2:9 NLT).

Several days after Pastor Dan breathed Jesus' words into my heart that Ash Wednesday night, I asked Eric for a copy of the blessing he had read over me. Surely, I thought, it was a prayer said through the ages, a blessing passed down through the ancestors of the church, memorized and recited over the hundreds of people who came to him that night. I had found encouragement in it, yes, but more so I was certain that God had spoken directly into my dreams, an inexplicable message to be faithful to the Stirring. I wanted to slather the words over every inch of my dwelling, to tie them as symbols on my hands, and read them again and again when I laid down and when I got up and when I walked along the road so that I could remember that God spoke, that he cared about my dreams.

Two days I waited for the answer, and when it came back, I was struck by the intimacy of a Father who incomprehensibly names, knows, and loves. For the answer that came back to me was not the citation of a rote prayer through the ages, not an adage from the legacy of church fathers or a paragraph from the Book of Common Prayer.

The answer came back with grace and love, a twist of the ironic.

"I asked Dan for the prayer he read over you," Eric said from the other end of the phone.

"And . . . ?" I waited.

"He said it was no prayer. He said those words had never been written down or spoken before that night. He said they were spoken only to you. He said he asked God to give him something for each person and those were God's words for you. Only for you."

I hung up the phone and sunk slowly to the steps beneath me, allowing the weight I felt for the first time in the basement of a church to overtake me. The sobs were immediate and visceral. Holiness had once again entered my deepest dreams. I sat in the company of Hagar, desperate and weeping under the tree, and experienced the God the Bible calls El Roi, the God who sees.

To me, the God who names.

11

Rushing

*Of all ridiculous things the
most ridiculous seems to me, to be busy.*

SØREN KIERKEGAARD

When I was a kid, everyone in the house knew they could get me to do anything they wanted with three simple words: *I'll time you.* (It wasn't until I was well into adulthood that I was first shocked, then crushed, to learn that no one ever so much as glanced at a clock.) All kidding aside (and there is still much kidding about it among my siblings to this day), a competitive spirit is part of who I am; feeding it was one of the best gifts my family ever gave me, growing in me an unbridled love of sport. Like most things we invest in, passion came first, passion begetting hard work, all of which would eventually culminate in a college track scholarship.

Only things didn't go exactly as planned.

In the early spring of my freshman year, at the three-quarter mark of a 400-meter sprint, I collapsed in the grass of the football field, the rubber track grainy under my heels, dark pellets clinging to the sweat of my calves, tears streaming, pain writhing. A bone scan revealed hairline fractures in both of my shins. I was handed a redshirt, immediately halting my ability to compete. Later that spring, my team would win the conference championship for the one and only time in my college career. I watched in my warm-up jersey from the fifty-yard line.

I'd call my dad during this time—the first time in my young life I felt the demoralization of failure, stripped of the part of me I had embraced the most, vacant of performance, questioning if I was really any good at the thing I was supposed to be good at. It was my first heavy-weight wrestling match with identity and significance.

My dad would listen patiently, and then the fibers would carry the reassurance of his voice back to me, always saying the same thing from the other end of the phone: "Keep plugging away. It will eventually pay off. Just keep plugging away." I took his advice to heart and each day mustered just enough courage to gather the shards of rejection and embarrassment and failure that were splattered like freckles on my skin and went to work—again and again. The next spring I'd earn my first of three All-Conference honors and, two years later, went on to be voted team captain by my peers.

Just keep plugging away. It will eventually pay off.

I still say it to myself repeatedly. Like every five minutes of every day.

My alarm goes off at 5:04 a.m.

My first thought is incomprehensible even to myself, nothing more than a loath-filled grunt. My second is a foggy inventory of my day, racing to pinpoint the moment I can drop into bed and lie here again.

I head to the gym and walk back through my garage door at 6:45 a.m. I flip on the coffee, shake the kids awake for school, and spend the next hour clumsily moving back and forth between parent and working professional. My morning, like every morning, is an intermittent to-do list, a scavenger hunt for clean socks and missing homework: Shower. Pack lunches. Put on make-up. Dig through dirty clothes for PE uniforms. Dry hair. Locate missing homework. Get dressed. Yell things from the bathroom door like "finish your breakfast," "brush your teeth," and "put on your shoes" (ad nauseam) as I straighten my hair. Throw back coffee and toast. At 7:15 yell, "Bus is here!" and give hasty kisses as the kids scoot across the street. Check myself: Keys. Phone. Wallet. Backpack. I'm out the door to catch the 7:55 Metra. Work, commute in reverse, dinner at 6 p.m., homework, mad dash for practice, church, meetings, writing, social engagements, whatever the evening holds.

Sleep. Grunt. Start all over again.

Like the crashing force of a cascading waterfall, I am a broken record of rushing noise, a perpetual cycle of busyness, chronically exhausted, except when I'm not. I am also a mirror: I look no different than most people I know. *Drowning* was the word I'd first used with my friend Carla when I'd asked her to mentor me nearly two years before and was the word in my pleading email she'd honed in on more than any other. The drowning, at its worst, is a throwback to hot summer evenings spent in swimming pools with teenage boys who'd dunk my head, pushing me down repeatedly, sputtering, before I could catch my next breath, an adolescent game I never thought was funny. The fear of being without air, even momentarily, has never brought me anything but panic.

Over breakfast one morning, Carla asks me when I rest. I do, I know I do, but I stare at her incredulously, like she just asked me to solve an eighth grade algebra problem without pencil or paper (not that it would matter), and I am unable to come up with a straight answer. *I rest,* I say. *I do.* And I mean it, but after a few fumbled attempts to come up with anything concrete, my words trail off. I'm as incapable of calculating rest as I am of solving the algebra problem.

The waterfall feels like it will never stop crashing. I try to muster enough energy to rise to the surface for a gulp or two of air before the uninhibited force comes crashing again, pushing me deep into waters where I don't belong nor want to be. My lungs burn as the undercurrent finds its way around my ankles, and I desperately seek the next opening where I can catch my breath before it pushes me down again. Perhaps what frustrates me most is that I'm not the kind of person who's wired for a hurried life. I actually abhor it. I live it out of necessity, scrambling to my feet to keep up with its incessant demands, often resigning myself to hurl my leftovers at the world. For the record, I don't think this is a good way to live. I'm not cut out for the rushing. I wonder how many of us really are.

And so I find myself longing for a slower pace.

Sometimes I blame my location, rationalizing that if I only lived somewhere life didn't move so swiftly, like in the country where I grew up, I could finally catch my breath. (On our first trip to Chicago, they'd scheduled Eric's interviews so tightly that they'd forgotten to feed us dinner. I'd come home with blisters on my feet after our "break" blitzing the outdoor mall.) My phone dings and my sister-in-law's photo stream shows a picture of my nephews tending what seems to me like their acre-wide garden, making homemade jam from blackberries they'd picked themselves. Yearning seeps as I fight the creeping envy of children being raised on the Farm in the way I wish my kids were, away from the concrete and strip malls and the endless registration deadlines of activities that give rise to the pressure of missing out and fear of falling behind always bearing down, despite how determined we've been not to get sucked into those lies. The Farm, where I can ingest long, sweeping breaths that fill my chest with air that is pure and clean, uncontaminated with the congestion of the suburbs, filled with the wings of fireflies, the pixie dust of milkweed, and the soft, fuzzy seeds of the dandelions that dance with the evening breeze.

Even in my utopia, I know it's a lie.

Geography won't contain the rushing. Rushing is a state of being, a manner of living, and it resides within each one of us. "In our rushing, bulls in china shops," says Ann Voskamp, "we break our own lives."

And it always seems to get in the way of the Stirring.

When I'm not blaming my geography, I tend to blame the season. In my current season: kids, husband, work—in that order.

But I've learned this as I look back at the seasons of my life: there's not been one that's been absent of the waterfall. I think back to a few years ago when Sadie and Clay were both finally in school all day. I dreamed of all the things I would do with my extra time, only to fill it so quickly that I felt like I never had enough. Then I thought back to when my kids were very little, the long days full of unending interruptions and playdough and PBS and then there was all the crying and how I couldn't think straight and couldn't find a minute to spend with myself or my thoughts and there was no way I had time to pursue the dreams in my heart or even know what they were because I was just so busy. And then there was the time when I was a young working professional, newly married, and we were just so busy.

"Time can seem like an enemy," Kathleen Norris says. "It chews us up and spits us out with appalling ease."

I take great comfort in knowing there will be seasons in my life where I'll be more available than others, seasons that ebb and flow, and I will change and flow with them, my time no longer dictated by the incessant ticking of the clock. I take comfort in it because it gives me hope that there will come a day when I can step out of the rushing. And so I hold on to the vapor of days to come when I'm sure things will change, where the continuum of time will open its doors, bend its knee, and finally curtsey. "You've made it," she'll say. "You now may do as you please."

But then I sit on my friend Jeannine's couch and I'm reminded of the lie once again.

Jeannine is a beautiful woman who makes space to listen to God; her easy nature and kind spirit are magnetic. I thought I'd have more time to figure things out when I retired, she says, but we're so busy. And there are so many ways I can spend my time, she says, I don't often know which way to turn. And I deflate every time I hear this from someone her age, because I've been so certain of the illusion that the future is surely where my respite lies. I dream of long days of leisure, hiking, writing, napping, a mile-high stack of books on a sunny patio with a sweating glass of iced tea. I imagine it never rains and it's never cold and I'm always happy, because what in the world could I have to be unhappy about in this sweet life of leisure and pleasure? And then I see actual people I know who are retired—the real ones—and all they talk about is how busy they are. Busy with projects and volunteer work and grandchildren and gardens and cruises through Alaska and the open sea. Jeannine interrupts my thoughts: "It's really interesting," she says. "I'm not sure what God is calling me to in this new season (i.e., I don't know what I want to be when I grow up), but I'm open to listening and figuring it out." I deflate even more. *Even beautiful and wise Jeannine hasn't figured it out by now?*

The most suffocating part in the midst of all the rushing is that I ache to live out my dream. I ache to feed the Stirring, to float on my back at the pace of a lazy river and follow it wherever it leads. To go to new heights, experience new depths, to take long uninterrupted walks; to sit in coffee shops, to read the great minds of literature and ponder the deep things of life; to spend quality time with the ones

I most love without feeling pressure to get to the next thing. To tear up the intermittent to-do list. To not be interrupted. To live only out of my sweet spot, the places where my gifts are celebrated and my limitations evaporate with the breeze of the dandelion seeds.

Altruistic and unrealistic, for sure, but still, when it comes to listening to the sound of my dreams, I long to be free of the seasons—all of them—and live out my passion without restraint. At my worst, every task of my day begins to feel like an obstacle to the thing I'm really supposed to be doing. And this is when I know I've lost perspective: I'm focused too much on the destination and not enough on the becoming. I've become self-absorbed. I'm so busy chasing the future that I miss the beauty of the present, and this is nothing less than tragic.

Yet, at the same time I believe in being attentive to the present, I also believe that our dreams both deserve and demand our attention; that our dreams and longings and callings deserve the very best part of our gifts and our efforts right smack dab in the middle of all the rushing. The paradox is maddening and, frankly, exhausting, but this is the tension we live within each frenetic day: Choosing the present. Choosing the future. Choosing to live out our dreams, to keep plugging away, while the force of the waterfall threatens to thrust us against the rocks and drown us entirely. Because if we don't live intentionally toward our dreams, the water will swallow us whole, and someday we'll look at the bottom of an ocean somewhere and see our souls left for dead on the lonely soot of its dark and depressing floor.

"Do not lose hold of your dreams or aspirations," says Henry David Thoreau. "For if you do, you may still exist but you have ceased to live."

A few months ago, I spent a Friday night tucked away in our home office with nothing more than my laptop and printer. I needed to get a handle on where I was with my writing and was weary of staring at too many screens. I needed paper. I needed a pen. I needed to *see and touch*. I spent more than three hours printing everything I'd written in the last eight years. I couldn't believe how many files I had; things I didn't even remember writing, things, at the time, I thought were simply a waste of time. I'd written many of them as I wrestled with the Stirring—some were fist-pounding rants about what God was or wasn't doing in my life, some were creative exercises, others were articles I'd published or pieces I was trying on for size that were, in the end, really, truly terrible.

But some of them were gems.

After I'd finished printing, I went through each document and did a word count, marking each page. By the end of the night, to my astonishment, I'd discovered I'd written more than 100,000 words over these last eight years. I started to cry. Malcom Gladwell would be proud.

Keep plugging away.

In the midst of all the rushing, I had taken the time I could, the nooks and crannies of my days and nights, the pieces of myself that I could muster in the midst of the exhaustion, and I wrote them down, I offered them to my dream. I wrote them to help me, as E. B. White says, to know what I think; I wrote them as prayers to God. I wrote them as a way of practicing my craft. I wrote them because even in the midst of all the ambiguity, I must have believed that I was supposed to; something inside of me kept pulling me back to work toward my dream.

Our biggest fear is that season after season will go by and we will be no further down the path than we were in season number one or two or three. That we'll end up at season eight and wonder what we've been doing all this time. And so in each season, regardless of the rushing, we fight to keep our dreams in front of us. We cling to God and beg for grace. And sometimes we must sleep.

Knowing what we want to be and being intentional about getting there are two different things. I think how many people want to become but don't have a plan, people that let the chaos of life push them around and get them off course, people that don't keep holding the dream out in front of them despite the crashing of the waterfall and continue to take small steps in the same direction until they eventually end up at the place they, by faith, believed they might end up.

12

Present

*We are called to be the steward not of some ideal life or
even the life we wish we had; rather we are called to
be steward of the life that we have on our hands.*

GORDON T. SMITH, *COURAGE AND CALLING*

In his book *The Rest of God*, Mark Buchanan tells this story:

Someone asked me recently what was my biggest regret in
life. I thought a moment, surveying the vast and cluttered
landscape of my blunders and losses, the evil I have done and
the evil that's been done against me.

"Being in a hurry," I said.

Pardon?

Being in a hurry. Getting to the next thing without fully
entering the thing in front of me. I cannot think of a single
advantage I've ever gained from being in a hurry. But a
thousand broken and missed things, tens of thousands, lie in
the wake of all that rushing. Through all that haste, I thought
I was making up time. It turns out I was throwing it away.

I didn't know her that well. My grandmother, that is. Several years ago, she lay dying in a hospital bed and I wondered if I should get on a plane to see her before she died.

Ellen Mae was the wife of a World War II vet who also happened to be a bona fide alcoholic. Every other summer, my parents would wake us at 4:00 a.m. and pile us, blurry-eyed, into our Dodge minivan, the one with the 1983 Apache camper hitched to the rear, and drive west to Wichita where my mom grew up and later met my dad. My dad landed at Wichita State on a football scholarship, taking a train from the Farm after never having been further west than Kentucky, while my mom got a scholarship for her grades, eventually becoming the editor of the college yearbook. He was her third date of the day and, thankfully, the one that stuck. Those every-other summers were largely the beginning and end of my relationship with my grandparents.

We'd often spend the week at the house of my parents' best friends, daily making the drive across town to visit my grandparents, a largely perfunctory task. The four of us kids would awkwardly crowd in the living room, me always sitting on the floor at my grandfather's feet and, for what seemed like hours, listen as he talked. It's only now as I reflect back, when I really try to recall the memory, that I realize I don't know what his stories were about. Politics, war, history, articles he was reading perhaps. I mostly remember the stacks of books that surrounded his elbows, an aluminum TV tray next to his chair, and the two Siamese cats who were forever perched precariously about the room, scowling at the inconvenience of our presence until we'd finally tuck our tails to leave. And I remember how surprised I was when, in the midst of one of his stories, my grandfather would call one of us by name, because I wasn't convinced that he actually knew them. Sometimes I held my breath because I was certain he'd get us all wrong.

Although my grandfather quit drinking cold turkey in 1970 after a visit to the doctor revealed cirrhosis of the liver, the relational damage had largely been done. As I got older, I picked up fragments of my mom's story—how she'd spend summers at a camp paid for by her Nanna (Nanna with two "*n*'s," just like my kids call her now), an escape from a house she didn't particularly care to be in; how she'd come home from college after her first semester to find he'd sold her beloved piano without her permission; how, in all the years she worked to become a nationally ranked speed skater (in the 1950s, nonetheless, in the days before women were deemed capable of dribbling the length of an entire basketball court or running a marathon) her parents never once saw her compete. And how they'd never come to visit us out at the Farm—never once in all the years I remember, and how it wasn't until after my grandfather passed away, after I'd had my first child, that my grandmother finally made the trip.

And so as my grandmother lay dying, I debated whether or not to book my plane ticket, like I was debating the cost-benefit ratio of buying a new couch.

When I lament the rushing, when I lament the dishes and my job and the kids' schedule and Eric's work and his graduate school and the crashing of the waterfall because I just want to be attentive to the Stirring, Eric says things that annoy me. The present, in fact, is one of our most recurring arguments, like how we argue about him always leaving the garage door open or how I can't seem to pull the car in the driveway without maligning half the front yard.

He says things like, "The biggest problem with people today is they think they have to have it all right now," or "You know, Moses waited forty years to go back to Egypt and he never did get in the Promised Land," or "One of the biggest challenges in our culture, and for you especially, is that we have to learn to chase the future while still being faithful to the present."

Oh, wait. That's a good one—and the one that annoys me the most.

I know that the present is one of the most beautiful gifts we've been given. The present is where life unfolds, when we're focused more on who we're becoming than on where we're trying to go. The future can't shape us because it has not happened yet; only the present (which also will, at some point, become our past) can shape us into who we are. While the past reminds us who we are, the sanctifying process of the present whittles our character and our holiness to allow us to see each day as a step closer to the divine.

Yet in all the rushing and hurry, the present is what I begin to resent the most.

The present where my children, the two most beautiful and impressionable souls I know, live in the shelter and protection and guidance of my home, a home that will only contain them for a handful more years. The present where all four of my children's grandparents are vibrant and healthy, where I can still wear four-inch heels, and I have a life I largely I love. The present where I learn to become a better writer, where my marriage heals and grows, where my friendships run deep for the sheer quality of time and experience we've communed together; where I am finally learning to accept myself and those around me, flawed and broken as we all are; where pretense becomes intolerable, image-keeping laughable, where a few extra pounds around my waistline aren't the end of the world, where sunscreen becomes more important than the bronze of a glowing tan. The present, where I've become a person who listens better, talks less, lives and loves more intentionally; where interruptions become invitations, where I recognize my perpetual need for grace, and where eternity becomes the only answer that makes sense of this unjust and broken world.

The present, where becoming happens in the thickest parts of all the doing.

It is fall, and I am cleaning my backyard, pulling weeds, pruning bushes, digging through the earth of my flowerpots, clipping burnt ends. From the top of the yard, I can see the patio furniture resting on the bricks at the bottom of the gentle slope of the yard, the tiki torches surrounding the oval table that is now dusted with pollen, and a hollow feeling gnaws at the pit of my stomach. Another summer gone. Why didn't I pull the bushes in the corner and plant the azalea that I'd been meaning to plant (for the fourth year in a row)? Why didn't I string lights through the trees, *again*? Have we sat still enough, soaked in enough sun, enough stars, wiped enough sweat? Extended enough invitations? The worn fence needs a new coat of stain, weeds spill over the side of the artificial pond, a scrap of paper has blown against the side of the house and stubbornly tucked itself in the hostas.

I step on a small yellow ball, an accessory to Clay's pitching machine he'd gotten for his birthday earlier that spring. I pick up a bucket, tilt the lid so the water slides off, and place the yellow ball, tenderly, inside. I move toward the shed and this time find a real baseball, waterlogged and worn. I squeeze its threads hard as I look at his machine, broken in the corner, and I smile. And I ache. The hours my son has spent in this yard with a ball, not one second of their ticking ever to be returned. Now the yard is too small; it can barely contain him. Tears sting my eyes.

The present is the most challenging to navigate in the thick of the Stirring.

My friend Ed once told me that we spend so much time wondering what we're called to that we forget we're called to whatever we're doing right now. This I needed to hear, for the present is not a barrier to our call. It is our call.

"One common problem for people who believe that God has one particular job in mind for them is that it is almost never the job they are presently doing," says Barbara Brown Taylor in her book *An Altar in the World.*

> This means that those who are busiest trying to figure out God's purpose for their lives are often the least purposeful about the work they are already doing. They can look right through the people they work with, since those people are not players in the divine plan. They find ways to do their work without investing very much in it, since that work is not part of the divine plan. The mission to read God's mind becomes a strategy for keeping their minds off their present unhappiness, until they become like ghosts going through the motions of the people they once were but no longer wish to be.

These thoughts were revolutionary for me in the same way the missionary told me we were first and foremost called to God or the way my friend Adele would later ask me who I wanted to be. It became like a leather strap woven tightly around my ankle, tethering me both to the present and to the divine in a way that has kept me from tossing in the wind, bringing contentment and peace when I needed it most. Because God is not some *thing* we chase after in hopes of a more sane life, God is the present, holding our hands each insane day.

I got on the plane, because when people are dying, you go. You choose the present.

I hadn't seen her in a handful of years. And so now it was midnight and I stood next to my grandmother's bedside and realized how ill-prepared I was for seeing someone hours from death. Her body lay shriveled in a cotton nightgown under an even thinner cotton sheet, her mouth parted in a small *o*, her head tipped backward, her chin almost straight to the ceiling; her hair brittle, her breathing labored, the uneven intakes of oxygen murmuring the imminence of death.

I whispered in her ear like we were old friends, like we shared a history of intimate conversations over tea parties and sleepovers that ran deep over the years. I stroked her hands and her forearms; I told her that I was there, that she was going to be okay, that Jesus was waiting, that it was time for her to go. I told her she was safe. I told her I loved her. I cried. I prayed. I softly said goodbye and gave her permission to let go, as if she had been waiting for me to come. Had I known her, I think I might have found her to be a beautiful woman. Regret floated through my tears, a reminder that the present shouldn't be seized only in the face of last-chance moments.

Four hours later, my cell phone buzzed on the nightstand, awaking my sister Bobbi and me to the reality of death. We sat on the edge of the bed and, in the dark quiet of the room, cried for a woman we'd only ever known from a distance. The next forty-eight hours were filled with moments I suppose are typical when a family gathers to mourn—listening to stories I'd never heard, seeing photos of ancestors I never knew I had, having uninterrupted conversation with relatives I hadn't seen in years, reliving snippets of lives I didn't know existed.

But it was the unexpected moments, the kind we can't anticipate or plan for, that gave way to the fullness of the present, the realization that when we hastily wonder if the cost will be worth tossing aside our selfish inhibitions to choose the present, the answer, without fail, is yes.

Its full weight bared down as Bobbi and I sat in the back seat of a car, my parents our tour guides as they shared their first years of life together: their first apartment, the house where my sister spent her first sleepless night, the river next to my mom's high school where she won (repeatedly, she assured us) the annual regatta; the school where my dad held his first job, the park where they used to walk, the big yellow boarding house where they lived when my dad played minor league baseball for the Minnesota Twins, and, my favorite, the story of the home's Italian landlady whose heart my mom stole so completely that she gave up her secret family pumpkin bread recipe—a recipe that, to this day, I don't live through a Thanksgiving without.

Oh, there were more. Reconnecting with friends who were like cousins growing up, walking into a house that felt like home after years of playing host to sweet summer vacations, reading letters my mom had written from summer camp when she was ten (not just reading them, but seeing her childhood penmanship), and watching my parents, after nearly fifty years of marriage, be there (I mean really *be there*) for one another as my mom said goodbye to her mother, the last living parent either of them would know.

When I left on Sunday morning, I had no regrets. I hugged my family at the airport, my heart brimming with the things I would have missed had I decided to choose the easier path. The easier path would have cost me less, sure, but would have left me wondering, restless, and void of the fullness that only comes when we abandon our indecision and choose to say yes to the present.

The morning my grandmother passed away, a nurse grabbed me as I was leaving her room. "Your grandmother," she said, "was a sharp-witted lady with a very soft heart." After my weekend in Wichita, I have no doubt that was true.

We come to these moments, in the midst of all the rushing, in the midst of being intentional, when we wonder if we should choose the present. If we should go when we're too busy, when life is dragging us by the back of the shirt, pulling us like a rag doll tied to the bumper of a car as we desperately try to get our feet under us and somehow slow the whole thing down (but instead we're at the mercy of the bumper and the rope and the speed of the car). Moments when we're trying so hard to be intentional about where we're going that we lose sight of where we already are; when we forget that life is a marathon not a sprint. Yet the present always propels us toward our dreams because our dreams are built in the midst of it.

And the present is always, always, part of the becoming. It prods us on the journey, giving us the sounds we'll eventually come back and listen to, as it makes us more and more of who we are.

13

Ordinary

A deep fear in human life is being
trapped inside a too small story.

Andy Crouch

once gave a friend an essay I had written for a scholarship
to a writing conference, asking for feedback, in which I said I
wanted to change the world. She blithely scribbled a comment
in the margin, and I could hear her patronizing voice: "Don't you
mean 'your *corner* of the world'?"

I immediately became a little surly.

No, actually. I meant the whole world, and I was offended that
she, or anyone for that matter, would suggest otherwise.

At the time, my corner felt small, dingy, laced with cobwebs, gray
like overcast skies in the Midwest compared to the brilliant blue
that overlaid the ocean of the world. The weight of the calling I felt
on my life, the power of the Stirring, didn't merit a dusty, basement
corner that no one would ever see. It merited the whole world.

In the years since that essay, in the years that God has been
working out all my doing and becoming, my perspective has

changed. For in the pursuit of trying to change the whole world (not that I had a remote possibility at this), I've often been left hollow, never feeling quite big enough or accomplished enough no matter what things came my way. The famous words of J. D. Rockefeller, the first billionaire in American history, rang true when it came to my dreams. "How much money is enough, Mr. Rockefeller?" a reporter asked. "Just a little bit more," he replied.

Just a little bit more.

Because in our pursuit of believing we can (or need to) change the whole world, we often miss the beauty in our own small corner. And I've come to really love my small corner.

My second best friend's house sat in the middle of the .14 square miles that officially marked the borough of Hookstown, Pennsylvania, a small town founded in the late 1700s, according to historical records, by two salt dealers and Revolutionary War heroes, brothers Matthias and Benjamin Hook, who left their home in Maryland to find land "in the wilderness of a new country along the Ohio River."

Like most kids I grew up with, Missy had a spacious yard with lush grass and tall evergreens. We'd spend hours climbing the limbs, swinging our legs as we talked about school and teachers and friends and boys, our time always culminating in one courageous leap from the highest branch we could dare. The town playground, the one with the frayed basketball hoops that sat across from the old white church, was adjacent to her house and was separated by a chain link fence with one small opening that we could wriggle through. During sleepovers, when one of us had to pee, we'd get up in the middle of the night and creep outside by the light of the moon to her family's outhouse. The bizarre thing was, I never thought it odd, even in 1985.

According to some historical records, in its infancy Hookstown was a flourishing village of 350 people, listing two tanneries, two blacksmith shops, a wagon maker, two tailors, a couple of hatters, a woolen mill, and some other small businesses. Thirty-three miles northwest of Pittsburgh, it was a stopping place for many, especially drovers moving livestock from Pittsburgh to market. Today, according to the US Census Bureau, it boasts 151 souls.

To me, five hundred miles away in the country's third largest city, it was and is and always will be home. The place where all three of my schools—elementary, middle, and high school—sat on the same property, the same school where my parents were both teachers and my dad's mom before him and the football stadium is named after my dad. It was the place where you ran barefoot all summer long, fished for salamanders and crawdads in the creek, and rode your bike through miles of backcountry roads without thinking twice about a rogue stranger lurking in the woods. It's the place where hay is farmed in the summer, boys ride tractors to school on the day of the prom, high school football marks everyone's Friday nights, and directions are given by the names of landmarks and people's homes rather than state route numbers (go past Barrett Hill till you get to Laughlin's, then turn left toward Ponderosa at the Corners—that will take you out to Star Lake).

Every few years, however, the dark and windy roads tragically claimed the life of a classmate who was driving a little too fast a little too late at night, or was the victim of someone else who was. A wreath of flowers, often encircling a cross, always marked the side of the road, and sometimes, even years later, still does. Even now, when I go home for a visit, I drive by certain bends in the roads, and, without fail, the name of a classmate, sometimes years ahead or behind me (in a small town the years press together like the folds of an accordion), imprints on my mind. Dane. Scott. John. Mike. I knew all the spots because tragedy has a way of marking bends in the road, even when the tragedy isn't our own.

Tragedy in the deepest sense of the word has escaped me to this point in my life, leaving me with the vague and uneasy sense that eventually the other shoe will drop and someday it will be me. Someday I will be the one standing next to the hospital bed, picking up the phone in the middle of the night, crashing to my knees as I hear the results. I know it's true because it's inevitable. One day we'll all have our turn.

But in some twisted and warped way, I often lament the fact that I'm still awaiting my tragedy. Captivated and transformed by books like Jeannette Walls's *The Glass Castle* and Frank McCourt's *Angela's Ashes* and Mary Karr's *Liar's Club* and Laura Hildebrand's *Unbroken* and the way the depth of their stories cements themselves to me, stirring places inside of me that can only be stirred when someone has lived the kind of epic and tragic lives they've lived, I wonder when it will be my turn. Only I foolishly pray it won't hurt too much. But as my friend Christen chides me, in reality, it will always hurt more than we think; in fact, it will most likely swallow us whole and spit us out only once it's proved most inconvenient, covered in the dripping filth of its slime and spit with little regard for the limp pile we've become or how difficult it is to move on.

Each time the movie *Shawshank Redemption* comes on, I immediately become glued to the TV. It doesn't matter what I'm doing, how much time I don't have to watch it, the piles of laundry that surround me or the stack of bills that are unpaid or the number of emails left to return or the gargantuan weeds overtaking my flowerbed—I stop what I'm doing and I become a statue in its unfolding wake.

It has the classic elements of story that we all love, elements that make stories great, the kind of story that imbibes in its audience the universal truths of all of our stories: loss, grief, community, injustice, pain, heartache, joy, all wrapped in a character that we not only can't help but love but want to be ourselves. The best part is always the climax, the part where the protagonist overcomes indescribable atrocity to triumph just before the credits roll.

As the movie comes to a close, Andy Dufresne finally gets his triumphal ending after two decades of being imprisoned for a crime he didn't commit. After his creative escape, which included inching his way through a sewage tunnel, his best friend, Red, played by Morgan Freeman, closes the movie in perfect soliloquy, "Andy Dufresne crawled to freedom through five hundred yards of foulness I can't even imagine, or maybe I just don't want to. Five hundred yards . . . that's the length of five football fields, just shy of half a mile."

Yet as much as this story captivates me, the problem with it is the same problem with many of the immortal stories of our time: it reinforces our belief that these are the only stories that matter. Without a great trial to overcome, without going into the depths of the trenches covered in murk and mud and crawling through the sewage to get to the other side and having our moment to stand in the rain and be set free, unless we've done all that (and have done it infinitely low and incalculably high), our story simply doesn't matter all that much. It's not worth sharing because the great tragedy hasn't fallen on us; it's really not worth anyone's time. Our stories don't carry much weight, because they are somehow less authentic than someone who has been to greater depths of suffering or achieved greater success. And in all our disbelieving, our own story and our own Stirring shrink to such a place of inadequacy that they become too small even for our little corner.

Author Andy Crouch says the deepest truth of every human community and of every human being is a quest for a bigger story.

The drive to be of significance and meaning is as powerful as the basic human instincts toward hunger and avoidance of pain. A big enough story tells you how your life can be part of something significant and so we are continually asking the question "Is there a bigger story?" It's strange how often we find that the more successful we become in the "almost big enough stories," the smaller our stories start to become.

But what if part of the tragedy of this life is not seizing our small corners because we're waiting on the whole world? What if tragedy is not living out who we really are in a way that gives our very fullest and best selves to the very places we most spend our time? What if, for just this small space in time, we defined tragedy as not having the courage to take the risk we knew we should have, as never living out the things we thought we were most called to do, or the things that brought the most life and light into a dark and shady world? What if we set aside death and abuse and war and suicide and defined tragedy, just for this one selfish moment, as never becoming who we were fully meant to be? What if our dreams are not about experiencing grand or great or tragic things, or doing something extraordinary, but rather being faithful to the lives that we are actually living, our corners of the world, the ones we slug through each and every day?

In going after the whole world, we often shrink back in fear; we compare ourselves to death with others; we let insecurity and doubt become the voices that lead us rather than stepping into who we fully are. Accepting our gifts and talents and stories as extraordinary because no one else can combine those with our own personal story, our experience, our own sense of tragedy and loss (whatever that may be), our accomplishments and celebrations, our small towns and our big cities, our homes and our families and all the things that go into making us who we are.

In Donald Miller's *A Million Miles in a Thousand Years*, a book about living a better story, there's a scene that makes me laugh out loud every time I read it. Don's in conversation with two movie executives, Steve and Ben, who are trying to make his life into a movie based off of the success of his best-selling memoir *Blue Like Jazz*. They, along with Don, are staring at a whiteboard trying, rather unsuccessfully, to come up with the story arc. Don tells this story:

Steve sat thoughtfully and collected his ideas. He scratched his chin and collected some sympathy. "In a pure story," he said like a professor, "there is purpose in every scene, in every line of dialogue. A movie is going somewhere."

The last line rang in my ears like an accusation [Don speaking]. I felt defensive, as though the scenes in my life weren't going anywhere. I mean, I knew they weren't going anywhere, but it didn't seem okay for anybody else to say it. I didn't say anything; I tried to think about the philosophy of making movies so my face would look like I was thinking something other than the fact that Steve didn't think my life was going anywhere.

"What Steve is trying to say," Ben spoke up, reaching for the jar of olives, "is that your real life is boring."

"Boring?" I blurted.

"Boring," Ben repeated.

"Boring," Steve reluctantly agreed.

I thought about it for a second and then told them about the time I jumped off a bridge, and another time I saw a bear in the woods. "Those times weren't boring," I said.

"What happened with the bear?"

"He got spooked and ran off," I said.

"Oh," Ben replied, raising his eyebrows as though to confirm that my real life was boring. He pointed the jar of olives at me.

"No thank you," I said.

In the context of the book, the exchange makes me laugh. It's a brilliant little piece of writing. But in the context of real life, it makes me sad because I think it's often how so many of us feel, the fact that our lives are boring because we can't make them sound extraordinary to others.

But ordinary is all a matter of perspective, for a life doesn't feel ordinary to the one whose life it has impacted, the one who has been changed by the small dreams of a person who invested into their own dream. A life that follows the Stirring and chooses the becoming is never an ordinary life. Because the truth is, if we look at the nature of sin and humanity and the redeeming love story of God, we all have crawled through the sewage, been covered in the filth of a thousand murderers and thieves, and we've had our moment to stand in the rain, washed clean and free from the depths of our humanity by the beauty and grace of God.

> For all have sinned and fall short of the glory of God, and all are justified freely by his grace through the redemption that came by Christ Jesus. God presented Christ as a sacrifice of atonement through the shedding of his blood—to be received by faith. He did this to demonstrate his righteousness, because in his forbearance he had left the sins committed beforehand unpunished. (Romans 3:23-25)

And this is an extraordinary story; this is the story that gives us purpose, which makes all of our stories worthwhile and extraordinary and compels us to make a difference—in the whole world or just in our small, beautiful corner.

One Sunday morning, Eric and I made our way to his office after church. I was staring aimlessly out the window, waiting for him to pack up his things, when the red flashing of his voicemail light caught his attention. He pressed the button, putting the phone on speaker, and played the message aloud as he put his laptop in his bag. It was a voice we hadn't heard in fifteen years. A young man he'd mentored in a junior high small group back in Pittsburgh at the first church we, newly married, ever called home. Unbeknownst to us, he had become a pastor and was leading his first church. "This morning I challenged everyone in my congregation to call one person who has made a difference in their lives," he said. "You are my phone call. You listened to me and taught me and spent time with me. Thanks for taking the time to invest into me as an awkward and goofy junior high kid. You made more of a difference than you'll ever know."

We stared at each other in disbelief, me wiping the tears from the edges of my eyes.

The impact of a story, the influence of a life, does not lie in the grandness of it, but in the lives of those it touches.

"And once you live a good story," Miller says, "you get a taste for a kind of meaning in life, and you can't go back to being normal; you can't go back to meaningless scenes stitched together by the forgettable thread of wasted time."

As moved as I was by the call, I instinctively got a little sad, just like I get sad after I laugh at Don's exchange. I tried to think of one person who would pick up their phone and leave me that message. Maybe they were out there, but I couldn't come up with one.

14

Comparison

You are like no other being ever created since the beginning of Time, you are incomparable.

BRENDA UELAND, *IF YOU WANT TO WRITE*

I walk to the train several mornings a week, a commuter train that takes me to the city for my actual job. Actually, I walk from the parking lot to the train, but some days it feels like I've walked all seven miles from home instead of three hundred feet across the lot.

A few months after I accepted the admin job at the publishing house, a marketing position opened up that was more suited to my background, so I took it. About two years after that, I moved into a role as an assistant editor, which is the job I wanted three years earlier when I first applied for the internship. While I enjoyed my work, every time I had lunch or breakfast or coffee with an author, I couldn't help but get the overwhelming and regretful feeling that I was sitting on the wrong side of the table. I started to pray, hard, as I so often did about the Stirring, pleading to God for the millionth time to show me what he wanted me to do with my life.

A friend, who also happened to be my boss at the time, graciously walked me through an exercise that reflected back to me the highs and lows of my vocational life. One thing became clear: I wasn't living out of who I was. He saw it more clearly than I did, and the meeting became one of significant naming for which I will always be indebted. I cried my way through it like an idiot, right in the middle of a crowded Starbucks, and apologized a million times. I came home to an empty house and got on my knees, folding myself over the living room couch, exhausted from years of wrestling with the Stirring, overwhelmed by the intimacy of being known. I poured myself out as an offering to God to take my life and do with it whatever he wanted. Then I stood up and made dinner.

Almost exactly four months later, I'd have dinner with a friend who'd randomly mention a job opening that we both immediately knew I'd take. I left the publishing house, accepting a position at the nonprofit in the city that I currently work for, which is why I was now walking across the parking lot to catch the train. While I would enjoy many things about my new job, it would prove to be another experiment in trying to fill the Stirring with a vocation—a pilgrimage that, for me, would always prove hopelessly futile.

The trains, when they're working, operate on a rigid schedule, which means being one minute (or ten seconds) late can wreck your entire day. I know because I've been left heaving and sweaty on an empty platform, glaring at the conductor like he had something to do with it, more than once. On this particular morning, however, the time gods were on my side because I somehow managed to get to the station a full five minutes early. As I got out of my car, I quickly assessed how fast I needed to walk—down the street, a ninety-degree right turn past the dwarfed office building with the tinted windows, across the sprawling lot, under the cement overhang and up the stairs to the platform. I was about to pick up my pace, but I noticed no one else was moving particularly fast; in fact, no one seemed like they were in much of a hurry at all—no breathless steps, no anxious movements, no panic-stricken eyes in their coffee-laden faces. Everyone simply seemed to be taking their time.

It felt like the antithesis of the life I'd carved out in these fast-paced suburbs, and I felt a small murmur somewhere deep inside that longed for a life where everyone walked this slowly all of the time. And so I let myself relax. I exhaled. I slowed my steps. I let my watch rest at my side, and I matched the graceful rhythm of those around me. I lifted my eyes from the cracks in the pavement to the patches of white that smattered the sky. I inhaled. And I exhaled again.

In that moment it hit me how often I do this, how often I give myself permission to breathe more deeply when I see that everyone around me isn't pushing for every last second they can suck out of life. And how often I push harder when it looks like everyone else is doing the same, afraid I might fall behind if I don't. And I'm reminded of how often I'm guilty of paying too much attention to the speed and talent and beauty of others—their accomplishments, their gifts, their contributions to the world—and choosing to either speed up or slow down in an effort to match whatever pace they've carved out for themselves, rather than just moving along at the speed I had planned all along.

Despite the rushing, when it comes to meaningful things, I need deep and slow. I need a journey to process, memories to reflect on, pain to feel, people to connect with, moments to celebrate. I need to feel all that I need to feel before I can move on to the next thing. I create slowly. I don't like juggling too many things at once. I need balance and rhythm and rest. And because of this, I often find myself alone.

I often find myself wondering what's wrong with me, why I am wired the way I am or why I'm not wired like the people running to the train. I often find myself questioning if I've made the right decisions about my own path, evoking the gnawing restlessness of regret that bangs endlessly from one side of my mind to the other: if I should have taken that internship when others were writing their first books; if I should have grabbed the train to the city or invested more time helping others develop their ideas; if I should have at least tried sitting in a coffee shop writing my days away; if I should have let my brain ingest all that higher education had to offer instead of putting new windows in my house; if I should have hired a babysitter instead of taking a professional hiatus for all of those years.

The question at the heart of it all is this: *What if I'm living the wrong life? What if I'm not living the life I was supposed to live?* These questions are ultimately awful, because they cause us to believe that our decisions solely orchestrate the direction of our life. They put every scrap of sheet metal on the bed of what we do, and if the one thing we were supposed to do doesn't work out we somehow messed the whole thing up.

The sentences that start with *what if* are the most awful ones of all. I came across a 2004 commencement speech from American novelist Richard Russo, in which he tells a story of a colleague who sat in a puddle of tears because she was afraid she was living the wrong life. (It's an incredibly well-written story by the way, and one I'd commend every person to read.) He declares to the graduates that he tells them this story

> to suggest what the next decade of your lives is likely to be about, and that is, trying to ensure that you don't wake up at 32 or 35 or 40 tenured to a life that happened to you when you weren't paying strict attention, either because the money was good or it made your parents proud, because you were unlucky enough to discover an aptitude for the very thing that bores

you to tears, or for any of the other semi-valid reasons people marshal to justify allowing the true passion of their lives to leak away. If you're lucky, you may have more than one chance to get things right, but second and third chances, like second and third marriages, can be dicey propositions, and they don't come with guarantees. . . . The question then is this: How does a person keep from living the wrong life?

I adore my father almost more than any man on earth. Anyone close to me knows that the day he leaves this earth will be the day they come searching for me, pull me out of the back of a closet, and make me get dressed and brush my teeth and somehow go on with life. I'm not the only one who feels this way. Back around the Farm, my dad is simply known as "Coach" for all the years he spent at the high school, teaching and coaching and bringing out the best in kids that others had long written off, speaking far beyond any classroom or field, deep into the recesses of their lives. Still, in his fifteenth year of retirement, rarely a month goes by that one of his students doesn't reach out to him, intentionally, and tell him about the profound difference he's made in their lives.

He was my coach too.

Now, certain things we don't advertise about ourselves because we don't want others to get the wrong impression about who we are, but during my own high school years, I threw the discus, a small rubber apparatus hurled from a cement ring into a large open field, mostly by sweet and, if I'm being candid, broad, husky girls. The ironic thing was that I was a fraction of the size of most of my competitors, and yet my dad managed to coach me to three state medals. I'd stride into a meet and, based purely on my size, most people would assume I wasn't much of a threat. What they didn't know is that I spent hours upon hours spinning my feet in that ring, no disc in hand, in order to perfect my technique, and at the end of the day, that more than any brute strength is what made me win more often than I lost.

They say the past is the best indicator of the future, so you'd think after time, I would have learned to trust myself and the hours I'd logged, but regardless of any number of medals I strung on my wall, I'd always struggle with the shrinking insecurity that comes with feeling outmatched. I'd have to fight the temptation or, perhaps more accurately, the instinct to step into the ring, forget my technique, and instead use sheer force to heave the discus as far as I possibly could. Because anytime I didn't fight it—anytime I tried to buck up, muscle up, and rely on strength I didn't have to attempt what others did well instead of trusting where my unique adeptness lay—I'd epically and spectacularly fail.

This is how it is with comparison.

The harder we try to be more like whatever pieces of someone else we feel we should be more like, the worse it usually goes for us—and the more foolish we look. But knowing doesn't stop us from trying to heave ourselves in all the wrong directions (all it takes is one glimpse of the wrong reflection at the gym, one page of a book whose prose drips with cleverness and depth, one parent whose thoughtful and graceful way is so luminous we can't help but stare), and we're trapped under the weight of comparison's lies, wondering why we couldn't figure out how to throw some crazy apparatus farther than anyone else.

I confess in my own twisted mind, in the darkest places of my humanity, that I equate success for others with failure for me, especially when it has to do with the dreams that I want to claim as my own. I don't know why I do this, why I'm so susceptible to this particular vice (as irrational as it is), but I allow comparison to encroach so forcefully that it often rips my soul in two. The shards of one jagged side mature enough to celebrate others—and genuinely mean it; the other fragment squashed under the tonnage that believes I'm less than. What's worse, when I confess comparison it forces me to confess jealousy (which only adds to the weight because then not only do I feel pathetic and insecure but I'm admitting the general lousiness of my personhood as well) because the two go hand in hand. "Sometimes this human stuff is slimy and pathetic—jealousy especially so," Anne Lamott says. "I know that when someone gets a big slice of pie, it doesn't mean there's less for me. In fact, I know that there isn't even a pie, that there's plenty to go around, enough food and love and air. But I don't believe it for a second. I secretly believe there's a pie. I will go to my grave brandishing my fork."

Oh how I squeeze that brandishing fork.

It's one thing to compare the size of our waistlines or our budgets or our homes with other people's, but when we compare our whole lives against theirs, when we compare "our insides to other people's outside," as Lamott says, it can be the death of all joy. Comparison is a persistent and insatiable evil, a black hole of inadequacy that always wins, always leaves us feeling empty, like we're never quite doing enough, that we never are quite enough. It feels as if we'll never accomplish enough to feed its eternal pit. It feels that way because we won't.

And so I've had to talk to God quite a bit about this ugly side of my soul. The more I've confessed, and the more I've offered myself to the becoming, the more he speaks into my falsehoods. As it turns out, he has much to say. In his sovereignty, he reminds me over and over again that his plan for my life is not the same as his plan for any other life. That he knows all my days before one of them came to be. That insecurity and inadequacy based on the qualification of others has no place in his kingdom. That my own limitations measured against the strengths of others don't equate to the abysmal failure of who he uniquely created me to be. And that, despite all my fretting, the world—anyway—was not created for me.

Life is an interesting combination, a delicate balance, of staring straight ahead—focused on our own lanes, our own dreams, our own ambitions and careers and families—and gazing at everything around us. The combination is needed; if we spend too much time in our own lane, we begin to isolate ourselves, becoming self-absorbed, living in a desert of self-inflation or self-defeat. If we spend too much time assessing our own lives against the successes and failures of others, we drive ourselves into a never-ending hole of despair, self-loathing, and never-enough-ness, always wondering if we're living the wrong life.

But that's no way to live at all.

Back in the days when I was competing, my dad quickly learned to recognize the signs of my comparison: the shifting insecurity in my eyes, the subtle slump in my shoulders, the tiny hesitation in my gait. When he saw me crumbling, heard the doubt in my voice because I was certain I couldn't measure up, he'd always say the same thing. He'd say it once: stay within yourself. And he'd say it over and over again. Some words skate by us without leaving so much as a scratch, but others have a way of sticking to us, of landing somewhere on us, of crawling up our arms and into our brain until they eventually lodge themselves into our soul in a way that helps us become who we are. Or at least a piece of who we are.

I repeated those words as I walked to the train, and I've repeated those words, like a balm to my soul, a thousand times in a thousand situations.

Stay within yourself.

When I let my dad's words settle over me, I'm reminded of the truth of my Father, and they swirl together like only truth can; they wrap me in grace and set me free, not only to be all that he's created me to be, but to be only who he's created me to be.

And then I'm reminded that I'm called to a person, not to a thing. That my soul is on a journey that's headed into eternity, not to a destination that ends with some dusty medal that clangs and clatters on some dented wall. That none of my decisions, no matter how small or how significant they may be, can thwart God's plan for my life. That he is taking my unique story and using it to make me more of who I am. And who I am is not the same as anyone else. "Since you are like no other being ever created since the beginning of Time," Brenda Ueland said, "you are incomparable."

And so whether or not I would have chosen to take the train to the city or sit in a coffee shop, go back to school or go back to work, I choose to believe that God is still working out his purposes in and through me on my way to the becoming with every crooked step, in every frenetic day. And so when the temptation comes, when comparison threatens, I take a deep breath and remind myself of all of these things.

Stay within yourself, I say.

And then I say it again.

15

Becoming

*For what you see and hear depends a
good deal on where you are standing: it also
depends on what sort of person you are.*

C. S. LEWIS, *THE MAGICIAN'S NEPHEW*

My friend Ed once said that everyone should learn to drive someone else's car. You know, the exasperating moment when you borrow someone's car for a quick jaunt down the street only to find your fingers fumbling over what should be familiar buttons and knobs. Something that used to be as simple as moving the seat up or turning on the windshield wipers in your own car now leaves you breathless with angst. You grapple for buttons, swerve while trying to turn on the radio, stretch for pedals that are inches out of reach, and resign yourself to cold air when you wanted hot. At first, it's all a bit frustrating.

But then, as you drive down the street, you settle in and become cognizant of how different things look. And you're pleasantly surprised. You notice the easy way the pillows rest on the wicker furniture that sits high on your neighbor's porch, the blooming spring flowers next to the park sign at the end of your block; you see that the hairline fractures on the edge of the road are in need of re-painting and that the post office flag is stately and vast. These things have been in the same place all along, but just a mere twelve inches or so adjustment in your vantage point and everything seems to have settled anew.

The first time I saw *Dead Poets Society*, I fell in love with the transforming power of words, both spoken and written, for what became the first of countless times in my life. Daniel Keating, played by Robin Williams, is the new and unconventional prep-school English teacher who inspires his students by calling out passion and meaning in their lives. Using the words of poets like Walt Whitman and Henry David Thoreau, he iconically implores them to "suck the marrow out of life," to take risks, and to contribute their verse to the world. He quotes Whitman in answering one of the recurring questions of life about purpose and significance: "'That you are here—that life exists and identity; that the powerful play goes on and you may contribute a verse.' What will your verse be?" And then, in a moment of sheer story-telling brilliance, he beckons his students out of their everyday seats, invites them to stand on his desk and drink in the room from a new perspective.

"I stand on my desk to remind myself to constantly look at things in a different way," Keating said as he twirls around. "You see, the world looks very different from up here. Just when you think you know something, you have to look at it in a different way."

Regardless of how it happens or what propels it, experiences that push us to a new perspective on the entirety of how we live our lives, how we listen to the sound of our dreams and the Stirring, are essential to moving us forward. They cause us to tumble into a mudslide, toppling end over end, until life is so jumbled that it could never possibly look the same again.

Sometimes we need to drive someone else's car.

We need to stand on top of the desk and twirl with our arms spanned wide.

When I first met Adele, I didn't think she liked me very much.

It was shortly after we moved to Chicago. Eric was getting acclimated to his new job as a pastor on staff at a five thousand–plus-member church, his pace furiously fast from the onset, while I managed things at home—disoriented, overwhelmed, and perpetually lonely. My emotional state was fragile to say the least, a realization that, in hindsight, probably hit its low point when grief overcame me (shivering and sobbing) in the frozen food isle of the local grocery store after not being able to find chopped spinach—yet another reminder that nothing in my life felt remotely familiar. What's more, I was desperate for friends. Really, *any* friends. Adele was Eric's colleague and a well-respected, well-loved pastor at the church we now called home. When her name came up in conversation, it was like people were talking about their best friend, therapist, spiritual advisor, favorite aunt, and college roommate all wrapped into one. *Effusive* is an understatement. I desperately wanted to have the same association, but, honestly, I didn't understand what all the gushing was about.

For months I tried to make a connection with Adele, to receive a sliver of the wisdom that so many were gleaning, to see what others saw, but she remained aloof—polite, courteous, and kind, but aloof. In the end, I did what I always do when I can't break down people's walls: I internalized the feelings, wallowed in self-pity, and dug my heels on one self-absorbed assumption: she obviously didn't like me.

You can imagine my surprise, then, when later that same year on a crowded Sunday morning, Adele and her husband, Doug, stood on the stage of our church with Pastor Dan, laying out an emotional story of hurt and reconciliation. Apparently it had been a very difficult year for them, especially within the walls of the church. It quickly and embarrassingly dawned on me that my insecurity about whether she liked me or not, shockingly, was not the thing that was most keeping her up at night. Welcoming the young, overly ambitious staff couple (still in the honeymoon phase of a new job) wasn't on the top of her priority list. *The world was not created for me.* She was being neither callous nor rude; she was simply doing the best she could with the emotional capacity she had.

That same Sunday, the one with the stage, she sought me out as I was pouring my coffee. She grabbed me by both shoulders and looked me square in the eyes: "I haven't been able to welcome you in the way I should have. I hope you understand. I just . . ." She stumbled for a moment. "I just couldn't. I'm really very sorry."

A couple of weeks later we sat at her kitchen table and, over a bed of mixed greens, the walls began to crumble. Now I understood the gushing.

We've been friends ever since.

Adele is one of those people who has an aura; she puts off something into the universe that draws people in and makes them want to be around her. She's a bit of a mystic; a contemplative soul who collects artifacts from around the world, leads spiritual pilgrimages to Italy, spends a week's vacation in a reclusive artist community, and wears jewelry that she's beaded with her own lanky fingers. Both the gift and the burden of being all of those things—a four on the ancient art of the enneagram—is that it makes people feel like they can dig deep into their souls and vomit their life on you. And so they do. Somewhere along the way, Adele wised up, most admittedly for the sake of her waistline: when people said "let's do lunch," she said "let's take a walk," which is why we were walking now.

Not for the first time in our relationship, I was sharing my perplexity over the Stirring, feeling like God was calling me to do something without knowing exactly what it was or how I was going to get there, like it was an actual destination I could find by dropping a pin in my GPS. The feeling was palpable, a literal smoldering in my chest that didn't leave me in the busiest moments of my most chaotic days. I could identify certain pieces of it—that I wanted to write or teach, for example—but rather than leaving me incandescent with anticipation, I felt murky, confused, and utterly lost. I was exasperated by not knowing what to do—if I should get a certain kind of job or a certain kind of degree, about why clarity often came so seemingly easy for everyone else and about how it all felt ecclesiastically self-absorbed and meaningless anyway. The leaves crunched under our feet as we walked up and down the wooded hills; I pulled my sweater a little tighter around my shoulders. I was desperate for answers. I wanted someone to tell me what to do.

Adele listened. And then she asked me a question that no one had ever asked me before: "Have you ever thought that maybe instead of asking what you want to *do* with your life, you should start by asking who you want to *be?*"

It was *so* Adele. (This is why people love her and also why I wanted to punch her in the nose.)

"Actually, um, no" were probably the words that stumbled out of my mouth, but inside, thoughts were cascading: *Are you even listening to me? I've got some things I want to do. Big things that involve big dreams with significant change-the-world implications. I don't have time to think about who I want to be.*

Funny how the things that irritate us the most are often the things that leave their deepest mark.

Long after the conversation ended, I couldn't get the exchange out of my head. I kept imagining myself sitting in a rocking chair, old and gray, under the broad roof of a rickety porch, the warmth of an afghan secure on my legs—rocking, rocking, rocking—wondering if anyone would stop by to visit, to offer a kind word because of the kind person I was to them; if anyone would bring me a bowl of soup because I had once made them a crockpot of stew; if a college student would stop by on their summer break and thank me for encouraging her to use her gifts, or a young mom would creak up the steps to say she learned to parent her children with grace by watching me love my kids. Or a married couple would drop by, hand in hand, and say they stuck it out for all these years because they saw the way Eric and I stuck together through thick and thin. Or if anyone would simply pull up a chair and rock their day away with me because I had done nothing more than take the time to rock through life with them.

Who did I want to be?

The more I mulled it over, the more I let it turn in my mind and soak in my soul, the more it began to change everything I was reaching for. It pushed me to the top of the desk and made me twirl, wings spanned wide, to see the world and the shadow I'd have in it, from a whole new perspective. Gradual dawning began: the purpose of the Stirring had always been to point me to the becoming.

And, I've come to learn, the Becoming always starts with God.

"The God I've come to know over my adult life," says Beth Booram in her book *Starting Something New*, "is a God who is more interested in the formation of my personhood than my personal comfort. He's more interested in who I am than the outcome or achievements of my life. His concern is whether through the circumstances of my life, I'm becoming more like Jesus as I become my true self."

My friend Carla sent me an article by *New York Times* columnist David Brooks called "The Moral Bucket List," in which Brooks beautifully reflects on the kind of people he most admires and what draws him to them—a musical laugh, a generous spirit, a listening soul. And then he says this: "When I meet such a person it brightens my whole day. . . . It occurred to me that there were two sets of virtues. The résumé virtues and the eulogy virtues. The résumé virtues are the skills you bring to the marketplace. The eulogy virtues are the ones that are talked about at your funeral. . . . Many of us are clearer on how to build an external career than on how to build inner character."

Who did I want to be?

I'd argue that even in this profundity, Brooks's assessment was missing something, for *character* can be a generic word. Character can be construed as simply trying harder to be better people, but as people of faith, it takes on a whole new meaning. If we only strive harder to be better people, we miss out on the mysterious workings of the inner life, sanctification, a call to holiness. We are called to something deeper and more transforming than simply being better people. We're not moralists or deists or therapeutic do-gooders. We're followers, and there's something more mysterious that happens in our inner life than simply trying harder to be better people on the way to figuring out what we want to do when we grow up. As Carla reminded me, we don't work on who we want to be for the sake of the eulogy, but for the sake of knowing and listening to God. It's God incarnate. It's love in the flesh. It's not about doing. It's about becoming.

It's all a bit mysterious.

But users beware: becoming who we are is hard, way harder than doing.

Becoming means we have to dig deep into some areas of our soul to see our flaws and admit them to other people. Becoming means we have to rip off bandages and feel the sting, look at those scars that have been there forever, just moving with us from day to day as part of who we are, and recognize that they still hurt, more than a little; in fact they're gushing with puss and blood and bacteria that are infecting the rest of who we are. It's so much easier to live in that place of adding notches to our belt and climbing to the next thing. It's so much easier to go out and accomplish something rather than sitting with the person we actually are, flawed and broken and ugly and pathetic as that most certainly is.

When I offer myself to the becoming, it forces me to admit that I'm selfish with my time, that I secretly fear others' success, that I'm prone to jealousy, that envy lurks in my soul; that I don't encourage enough, listen enough, call enough; that I often enjoy being lazy. It causes me to confess that I think more highly of myself than I ought at the same time I don't think highly of myself at all; that with my lips I profess forgiveness when wounds still pulse for healing at the dust of the cross. It causes me to confess that I'm unorganized and scattered and distracted, a mess regardless of how put together I want others to think that I am; that I don't read my Bible as much as I should and I don't talk to God the way that I want and I don't pray with my kids as often as they need; that I'm often late, usually unprepared, a tornado of frenetic activity each time I walk out the door. The becoming causes me to recognize my sin for what it is—part of me whose ashes will always struggle within—but it also forces me to listen, and by faith believe, that I still belong to the song of the redeemed.

At some point during all the incessant doing, regardless of all of our flaws, we have to realize that who we are is all we really have to offer. And offering ourselves to the world and our dreams and fully to the becoming is no small thing. We have to trust that we're enough because God alone is enough. We have to accept that we are going to fail at both the becoming and the doing, neither of which makes us failures ourselves. We have to trust in the exquisite beauty and inherent power that lie within the embers of grace so that none can boast, but all of us can rest in the opulence of his unconditional love.

In her book *The Cloister Walk*, Kathleen Norris shares her story of becoming a Benedictine oblate, a profession of monastic vows that, in no small way, would change the way she lived her life. "I knew two things," Norris begins her journey. "I didn't feel ready to do it, but I had to act, to take the plunge. I had no idea where it would lead."

She goes on to explain that the word *oblate* is from the Latin word meaning "to offer" and that Jesus himself was often referred to as an "oblation" in the literature of the early church.

"The ancient word 'oblate' proved instructive for me," Norris said. "Having no idea what it meant, I appreciated its rich history when I first looked it up in the dictionary. But I also felt it presumptuous to claim to be an 'offering' and was extremely reluctant to apply to myself a word that had so often been applied to Jesus Christ."

During a three-year period, she sorts out her "muddle" with a kind, patient monk who was her oblate director. "Finally I said to him, 'I can't imagine why God would want me, of all people, as an offering. But if God is foolish enough to take me as I am, I guess I'd better do it.'"

The monk smiled broadly and said, "You're ready."

The becoming allows us to boldly and unselfishly declare that we are ready too. Even when we're not.

16

Broken Dreams

The Bible nudges us toward the risk of wanting in a world that slowly leaks with disappointment. It challenges us to hold fast to the doctrine of God's goodness when life, like a reckless child, stubbornly heads in the direction of the street.

JEN POLLOCK MICHEL, *TEACH US TO WANT*

An orange flag flickers, rapidly, on the antennae of my car. I am following the procession, void of traffic laws, through four-way stops all the way to the cemetery. My friend Rebecca has lost her dad to a rare form of leukemia. The grief is compounded (for everyone, actually) by the fact that she buried her sister eight years earlier, the result of a virus gone rapidly and violently septic, at the age of thirty-nine. Sometimes grief can be especially cruel, and my lament was particularly heavy for Rebecca's mom, Phyllis, who endured the tragic calamity of burying her daughter and her husband in the same decade. The three women, two sisters and their mom, now huddled around the casket with their families, reality setting in that what began as a family of five was now a family of three before any of the children hit their forty-sixth birthday. It was December, it was frigid, and I was sad in my bones.

The car limps along in the procession, Eric's fingertips lying loosely over the steering wheel, me staring glassy-eyed out the window into the dreary Chicago gray, watching as others move obliviously on with their lives. I reflect on the same thing I always reflect on when I'm in the lineage of the orange flags, its gravitas never ceasing to amaze me: for one cluster of people time is halted, screeched to a stop, their lives shaken unmercifully like the cubes in a Boggle game, while for the rest of us, time mundanely marches on without much more than a second-hand glance of compassion tossed at those left in its treacherous wake. The rest of us keep moving on with life, on to our jobs, on to pick up our children and our dry cleaning and to get our hair done. We keep moving forward while my friend Rebecca lowers her dad's casket into the ground and her family figures out how to move on anew, taking their first steps into a world they've never entered before.

The death of a person we love is, most often, the thing we'd define as our worst fear. The thought of spending even one day on this earth without our spouse, our best friend, our parents or siblings, or, if I dare muster the courage—our children—makes us dizzy with incomprehension. Few, I think, would disagree. And so I find it bizarre that when people inevitably face the unfathomable, most of us are willing to sit with them for a little while; we'll fill their refrigerators and carpool their kids and rub their arms when we see them at church or in the grocery store, but invariably we begin to wonder—no matter how much we resist the thought— *how long is this going to last?* No matter how selfish we tell ourselves we're being, we slowly begin to resent our own inconvenience. "Pull yourself up by your boot straps," we say (which by definition, by the way, is an impossible feat), a national motto of false heroism. Our culture tells us to rush people through grief, tapping our feet while we secretly wonder when they'll "get over it" so we can all get on with our lives. Get over the loss, the sadness, the depression, the most helpless darkness they've ever known. I remember an author once saying that we never really get over grief, it just becomes part of who we are. When I think of grief in my own life, I know this is true. "You feel as though you will bleed to death with the pain of it," explains Dumbledore to an anguished Harry Potter. Despite the adage, time alone doesn't heal all wounds. Grief has to have its way with us if we're ever to have hope of moving on again.

My friend Eva is a divorce lawyer and one of the most generous people I've ever known. Her apathy for divorce, ironically, is the thing that makes her a successful divorce lawyer. Grief crashed into her life when she lost her fourth child, Matthew, at nine months due to a rare metabolic disorder known as Pompe's disease, and somewhere in the aftermath incurred the pain of divorce herself. For two years, Eva and I had dinner together once a week. One evening, over a bottle of Silver Oak, she told me of her disdain for divorce, letting me in on what I felt like was an insider's trading secret.

"So you're a divorce lawyer that doesn't actually think it's good for people . . . ah, I mean most people . . . to get divorced?" I said.

"Right. Divorce is horrible," she said. "No one should have to go through that kind of pain."

"I've heard people say it's like death," I said.

"Worse than death," she said quickly. "At least in death, the person you love is no longer moving and breathing in a world where you exist. At some point, you can come to terms with the fact that they're gone. But in divorce, that person is still alive, moving and breathing and going on with their life, yet you are no longer part of their world nor are they yours. In essence, they are dead to you. And you to them. Except they are very much alive. And to me, that's worse than death."

I knew it was true the moment she said it.

I think this is what it must feel like to grieve a dream, to live with the sound of its broken pieces echoing through our empty halls. In reality it is dead, a flame eternally extinguished, and we have to grieve it as deeply as we grieve the loss of someone we love, but at the same time, it's still walking around with us, ingesting the same air even though it no longer exists. We sit with our broken dreams, watching the orange flag flickering in the wind, and wonder why everyone else is able to carry on so effortlessly while we're staring numbly into the dreary gray, left shivering in the dark of a cold and empty room.

Maybe the only thing worse than living with the sound of your own broken dream is sitting with the sound of someone's you love and not being able to do anything about it.

From the time Eric was a boy, all he ever wanted to do was play baseball. Cliché I know, but irrevocably true. He spent every summer for the better part of his life devoting himself to the game. He was one of the lucky few for whom it actually paid off—a Division I college scholarship, the signing of a professional contract, minor league glory lived out of slimy motel rooms and stifling coach buses. He was living his dream. Until one day he wasn't.

During his third year of minor league baseball, unnerved by the most paramount hitting slump he'd ever languished through, he walked into his manager's office and asked where he ranked. The manager laid out his options: stick it out and hope things got better or obtain his release in hopes of a trade. Eric decided it'd be worth it to ask for his release, hoping to get picked up by another team, but the offer never came. Devastated, numb, Eric packed up his belongings in the back of his Ford pick-up truck and left the dream he'd carried with him since he was seven to be swept away with the At-lantic tide. He'd spent his whole life working toward and sacrificing for this dream—and got within a stone's throw of it—only to have it, at the rosy age of twenty-four, evaporate in one ten-minute meeting. And just like that, he entered a life he'd never waded through before. The orange flag flickered while the rest of the world moved on.

All of these years later, when the grief blows through the windows of our suburban house with the first blooms of spring—and from time to time, it still does—I feel the weight of it with him and I ache, for there's nothing more I can offer than a kind smile, a gentle touch, and a shoulder that says it's going to be—and actually in most ways, already is—okay. No matter what it is, when your first love dies, when it's no longer part of your life, you have to figure out a way to move on without the thing you thought you'd always have with you. The heart doesn't know the difference of how our culture weighs dreams, it only knows the brokenness it feels when its dream is vapid of life. And the heart weeps.

In her book *Starting Something New,* Beth Booram says this about the loss of a dream: "You feel a similar elusive emptiness and hollow sorrow as those bereaved a child, not the loss of human life but the loss of a vision that had captured and consumed your imag-ination for months, maybe years, a dream in which you had in-vested time and thought and prayer and capital."

To be honest, I have no more of an answer to the brokenness for Eric than I do Rebecca because I don't have an answer for grief. I'd say cut your bootstraps. Wallow. Wail. Lie in your bed, pull the covers over your head, and stay there as long as you need. Until you don't need to anymore. And then when you're ready, get out of bed, breathe in and out, and put one foot in front of the other until it doesn't hurt so much.

I remember Carla once reminding me that our dreams don't define us; they are not the totality of our personhood, she said, which is why it's so important to know our purpose—our deeper calling to Jesus and our part in the redeeming love story—apart from our dreams. I remember the missionary who told me we were first and foremost called to God. I remember the gentle and poignant reminder from Lauren Winner in her book *Still*: we are "small character[s] in a story that is always fundamentally about God." And I remember to focus on the becoming.

That helps.

And then there's the words of Jen Pollock Michel in her book *Teach Us to Want*, as she makes her own attempt to make sense of the brokenness of life. She postures us aright.

> The Christian story, centered as it is on the death and resurrection of Jesus Christ, is the only story for making sense of desire and loss. Not all is right with the world, this world. But our story isn't over yet. More will be written. And the resurrection of Jesus Christ is like a seed of hope sown into our stories of despair: it's the opening chapter of the new creation, where death and disease, sin and suffering promise to be reversed; where beauty and hope—life—will one day be renewed. This is reason to desire: to pray boldly and to believe that God wants to do good in the world, even if that good fails to be fully realized now.

That helps too.

I speak the truth of words like these into my own fear; I speak them into the bizarre dreams I have about the Stirring. I speak them over myself as grief, in all its capriciousness, threatens to crash into my dreams—for success is void of guarantee simply because we offer ourselves to the Stirring. I am reminded of this persistent fear when I find this written in my journal:

It's 8:34 p.m. and I'm sitting outside Starbucks, waiting for Sadie's volleyball practice to end over an hour from now.

Not only has this been a particularly busy month, it's been a particularly difficult one. Eric is weeks from finishing graduate school and, after four long years, I feel like I'm going to collapse right before the finish line. We are on opposite schedules, taking turns running the kids in opposite directions and both fighting for the space to finish what we need to get done, famished carnivores desperate to devour the same lonely piece of meat. Writing deadlines are looming; summer is less than a week away, and I feel my time, like the flame of a waning candle, being snuffed out from under me.

I stare at the cars in the parking lot, at the empty chairs in front of me, at the trucks buzzing by on the highway, and I wonder, frenzied, how I'm going to get this done. It's not just time; it's energy. It's the creative space to say something of value, something intelligent, something that could move a person's soul. I know I need to get some words down, but I feel like I did on the train with the present being so hollow; I just don't know what to say. And then it dawns on me: how I can I pull something out from something that doesn't exist? I look for relief but am not sure there's any in sight. I wonder, very seriously, perhaps for the first time, if there's any way I can actually pull this off. I wonder if I am doomed to fail. I wonder if the sound of this particular dream will crash and burn. And if it does, what am I left with then?

The orange of my own flickering flag flashes through my mind, and I wonder how I'd recover if I watched my dreams being lowered into the ground. I laboriously remind myself once again that when my thoughts are consumed in this direction I've placed too much power in the hands of the wrong thing. Carla's words come back to me: *your identity is not found in your dreams.* I'm beckoned once again by the becoming, and my perspective settles back into its rightful place—at least for this meager ticking of the clock.

I think of Eric and Rebecca and all the facets of broken dreams that have shattered in this world and remind myself that even if all of it crashed and burned, I'd eventually be okay.

"It's like having a broken leg that never heals perfectly—that still hurts when the weather gets cold," says Anne Lammot of grief, "but you learn to dance with the limp."

And so, yes, there's always that too.

17

Shame

*This was a step into darkness that I was
trying to avoid—the darkness of seeing myself
more honestly than I really wanted to.*

PARKER PALMER, *LET YOUR LIFE SPEAK*

Shame found me for the first time when I was about
seven years old.

I was playing blithely in a swimming pool wearing cut-off
denim shorts and, from the waist up, naked.

For what seemed like a good part of my childhood, I ran topless
around the Farm without giving it a second thought, despite the
fact that I was well past the age when this kind of thing might have
been remotely acceptable. On this particular occasion, I was in a
small town adjacent to my own, an area that covered two-tenths of
a square mile where my mom played softball in a polyester uniform
colored a hideous yellow and brown. My brother David and I rode
our bikes all over town while she played, knocking on doors to see
who could come out to play. We knew we'd hit pay dirt when the
house with the swimming pool on the dead-end street was full of

spirited bursts. Never a swimsuit in tow, I simply tore off my shirt and jumped in with nothing more than cut-off jean shorts, just like one of the boys. It never occurred to me that there was anything wrong with it until one unveiling moment when the blonde hair and braids across the street, several years my junior, showed up in her pink ruffled one-piece. *Covered.*

Shame came crashing down on me, one colossal bucket at a time, and then covered me, clinging heavy as I dipped low under the water, determined forever not to resurface any higher than my chin. It was the first time it dawned on me that not only was I dressed (or not dressed) inappropriately, I was actually naked. I wonder if this was not unlike what it felt like for Adam and Eve, moving along completely unaware that they were anything but adequately clothed until their eyes were opened and they realized they weren't. "I heard you in the garden, and I was afraid because I was naked; so I hid" (Genesis 3:10). And then the shame and the hiding and the covering up that followed.

For as long as they both shall live.

Shame found me wholly and completely a few decades later.

It found me on the heels of a phone call that I never imagined I'd receive, one whose revelations would unveil a set of emotional wounds I'd inflicted with my own sinful gait. It found me when I confessed to my husband and was forced to grapple with pain more searing than I knew existed. It found me as I crashed to my knees in the middle of my kitchen floor. It found me rocking in the arms of a friend as we sat huddled on her bedroom carpet, saliva dripping from the creases of my lips. It found me unable to stop my hands from shaking, even in the grasp of my safest friends. It found me drunk on the rug of my bathroom floor. It found me in every corner of my life, over and over again, for the next five years.

All these years in a church and it's the one thing no one ever told me: brokenness is the depths of a hundred sorrows, the weight of a million griefs. There are few or perhaps no other pilgrimages more raw or painful or difficult to endure. It's nakedness on parade, even if you are the only one who knows that you're intimately exposed, which, ironically, only intensifies the shame. Brokenness is an illuminating exposé that shines into the black places you never wanted to see, maybe never even knew existed, but there they are glaring back at you, revealing your own humanity in a way that thrusts you into an expanse of anguish because you finally had to admit that you're worse than you ever thought. For all have sinned and fall short of the glory of God.

It's one thing to hear what shame is, to listen to someone else define it, to hear it spoken about from the lectern or the pulpit or to read it benignly in the recesses of a college psychology book. It's another for it to take up residence in the places where identity and belief collide and watch, defensively, as it camouflages every pore of your soul, that is to say, as shame defines you. Truth listlessly wielded cannot fend it off. Brené Brown says that shame corrupts the very part of us that believes we're capable of change. For me, it corrupted the very part of me that believed I was capable at all.

As a church, we do a great job with people who have fallen before they come in, those whose tragic stories and painful pasts are nothing but a pin drop on a journey of epic transformation. Their stories are the easiest for us to celebrate; we throw open the doors, put the music on span, roast the fattened calf, raise the banner of grace. But we don't really know what to do with those that fall right in the middle of our crowded Sunday mornings, the vestige of powdered donuts still fresh on their faces. Our instinct is to cast them out in a moment of self-righteousness, and I understand, I do. I understand the consequences of sin and the disappointment of actions incongruent with a life of faith. But with one hand we pat ourselves on the back for gently reminding those on whom shame has so bluntly fallen about the graciousness of a God who forgives. "He works all things for good," we say. And with the other we usher them out the door, twisting the knife in a place we so kindly told them that God had effortlessly forgiven and forgotten "as far as the east is from the west" (Psalm 103:12).

But righteous indignation only feeds the shame. For it is in the fall when we need grace the most, when we need someone to set aside their own anger and frustration and disappointment, even though it's rightfully theirs, and to slide across the couch and let our sobs soak the front of their shirt. For the most beautiful acts of grace appear when the offender feels the gravitas of undeserving mercy, when a tender spirit tugs the satin of white gloves to the crooks of their elbows and serves them tea from a silver cup. This is the kindest act of all. For no one is immune to falling from grace—which, by the way, isn't even a thing. How can we, by definition, ever fall from grace?

Theologian Miroslav Volf cautions us against desiring a God who showers us with gifts without demanding anything in return. He rightly reminds us that Jesus wouldn't have spent so much time preaching about how we live in passages like the Sermon on the Mount, calling us to stretch ourselves to the supplications of a holy and righteous God, if it didn't matter at all.

"God doesn't just scatter gifts, smiling blissful affirmation of who we are and what we do no matter who we happen to be and what we happen to do," Volf says. "God also urges us to do this or not to do that. . . . God's face twists in the pain of disappointment and even frowns in angry condemnation when we fail to live as we ought to, bringing devastation to ourselves as well as to those around us."

A true and necessary statement, theology at its best, but God's face twisting in disappointment is not the first image that those trapped under shame need to invoke. Disappointment already abounds in every crevice of their frames. What they need, instead, is to be enveloped in peace that transcends the reality of their brokenness; what they need is grace. They need the fortitude of a God who ate breakfast with Peter in the sand of the beach, who protected the adulteress from the jagged rubble of an angry mob, who created messianic lineage with the likes of Rahab the prostitute, David the adulterer, and Ahaz the child sacrificer; they need a savior who will meet them in the basement of an old white church, holding their hands as they weep, all for the sake of introduction. For grace is the only thing that can bring us back to the surface, that can help us make sense of the truth and falsehood of holding the shreds of paper in both of our pockets: *You are but dust. The world was made for you.* Grace is the only thing that can lift our shame and remind us that brokenness is not a phase we must travel through, a sojourn to endure, but the essence of who we are, which is to say sinners set free by that very same grace.

"To live by grace," says Brennan Manning, "means to acknowledge my whole life story, the light side and the dark. In admitting my shadow side I learn who I am and what God's grace means."

For it is only by grace that we, when broken and naked and ashamed, can take one more step into the direction of our dreams. It is only by grace that we can feel the weight of our disqualification and find the courage to lift our chin above the precipice of the water and offer ourselves to the world once again. It is only by grace that we can finally heal from our brokenness in the most holy of ways, overwhelmed by our irrevocable need for a Savior, overcome with gratitude for this gift we don't deserve. It is only by grace that we can fall face down in torment at the cross, miry swamp to our thighs, sorrow abounding, the truth of how incapable we truly are resounding, and receive the purple garments of a righteous King.

In choosing grace—in grace choosing us—we choose to believe that despite all the disqualifying mess we've made of our lives, all the mess that is the truth of who we are, we are still, irrevocably, worthy of love, worthy of being called, worthy of being chosen and worthy to follow the Stirring. Because grace is not a lofty theological idea or quality to be obtained. Grace is a person, and his name is Jesus Christ.

"In a very real sense not one of us is qualified, but it seems that God continually chooses the most unqualified to do his work, to bear his glory," Madeline L'Engle says. "If we are qualified, we tend to think that we have done the job ourselves. If we are forced to accept our evident lack of qualification, then there's no danger that we will confuse God's work with our own, or God's glory with our own."

My friend Elisa comes to my church and preaches from her book *The Beauty of Broken*. As the host of the morning service, I have the privilege of introducing her from the stage. Elisa is a powerful and anointed teacher, a mentor and friend; a gift of relationship I've been fortunate to receive. Somewhere during her sermon she says that being broken doesn't disqualify us from God's call on our lives, and I feel something catch in the back of my throat. My hands begin the familiar tremble. I've worked so hard, so diligently, to assure myself of this truth, but hearing her name what I ultimately fear only irradiates my persistent struggle. The weight in my chest advances hard and fast; tears sting the recesses of my eyes. Shame is a pesky and insistent worm; he delights in my billowing inadequacy, my crumbling vulnerability—and he is as heavy as the weight.

But Jesus is there, too, sitting next to me the way he always does, benevolently, and the words I've heard him whisper time and time again quietly dance through my mind, for he's whispering them to me now: *Do you believe that I am who I say that I am?*

I submitted to this one long ago. *Yes, Jesus, of course.*

Do you believe that you are who I say that you are?

A sharp intake of breath, for this is a more difficult question to answer. My lips purse tight, conflicted, and the tears now come fast, hot, wet. I scarcely shake my head, confess my unbelief, will myself to belief despite my inner protest . . . and eventually succumb (like I always do) to the fact that if I answer yes to the first, the second leaves me no choice.

And so, weakly, fragile . . . *Yes.*

When Elisa finishes, the lights dim to a creamy haze and the musician delicately strums her guitar, her voice nothing short of heavenly.

Amazing grace, how sweet the sound . . .

The soft glow of the room, the rising beauty of her anointing, the veracity of the hymn, the whispers of Jesus in my ear, the poignancy of a community given over to worship bring the tears full force and, regardless of who can see or how embarrassed I feel, I am helpless in their flow. Grace has its gentle way with me, irenic and warm like the glow of the lights, and I am helpless, as I should be—as we all should be—in its iridescent wake.

Then a sudden quickening of breath, panic, for when the song ends, I have to step back onto the stage and usher the benediction. As the song quiets, the musician nods the slightest nod in my direction, an affirmation that it's now my turn, and I take one deliberate step, then another, until I'm standing once again in the center of the stage. My shoulders swivel and I slowly lift my face to the crowd. The tears are still flowing; I struggle to summon my voice. But when I look past the lights and catch the faces of those staring back at me, it gradually dawns on me that everyone else is crying too. Peace, comfort, calm. Shame is not as selective as I had come to believe. Brokenness is not reserved for only a small few. Isolation is disregarded, exemption out of play. For all fall short of the glory of God.

And are healed by his grace.

"Our life is full of brokenness—broken relationships, broken promises, broken expectations," Henri Nouwen said. "How can we live with that brokenness without becoming bitter and resentful except by returning again and again to God's faithful presence in our lives?"

And so return we do. Again and again and again.

18

Longing

*When do our senses know anything
so utterly as when we lack it?*

MARILYNNE ROBINSON, *HOUSEKEEPING*

Today I catch the 8:12 Metra into the city, one later train than I normally take. The train heaves and sways and moans, as it always does on these mornings, the bouncing back with a vengeance.

An hour earlier, my exercise class had gone long and felt especially hard; my sweat-soaked shirt had turned cold, leaving me to shiver with the chill of spring as I unloaded the dishwasher, scraped the crusty edges of a potato casserole dish still in the sink from Easter two days before. I lifted a grateful prayer for the hospitality of my friend Nicole, my longest standing confidante since we'd moved to Chicago. Married to a former Army Ranger, Nicole immediately empathized with the loneliness that looms when transplanted to a new place; like us, she and her husband Doug didn't have family in town, and so we often forged our own family for the holidays, a tidbit, for whatever reason, I was especially thankful for this morning as I absently turned the dish on its hind legs to dry.

Sleep eluded me much of the night before, and so instead of moving upstairs and beginning my next task, I sink languidly into the couch, sipping my coffee particularly slow, dread washing over me at the thought of laboring through a shower, fixing my hair, looking presentable to the world. I am simply too tired to rush.

My thoughts of Nicole and Easter drift to the aftermath of the biblical account of the resurrection. Along with my church, I just spent the last forty days building hard and fast up to the empty tomb: the dust and brokenness of Ash Wednesday, the sacrifices of Lent, the triumphal entry of Palm Sunday, the last supper of Maundy Thursday, the crucifixion of Good Friday, all culminating in the listlessness of the rumpled grave cloths on a glorious Sunday morning. And yet here I am, two days later, lethargic, fighting my way back to work, and wondering, as I always do after Easter, what it was like on the second day for those first disciples, reliving their own forty days, trying to comprehend fuzzy snippets of the im-manency that was ultimately to come—loss compounded upon loss, even if it was for the greatest good this world has ever known. I wonder what would stir in their hearts as they watched their king ascend into paradise. I wonder at the depth of their longing as they waited for the clouds to someday part again.

When we moved to Chicago in 2005, the national housing market was at an all-time high, Chicago ranking ninth among the most difficult cities in which to move. Coming from small-town Ohio, the sticker shock alone perpetuated in me a constant state of anxiety for two solid months. I became convinced that we'd never be able to move—until finally our realtor, a seventy-something spitfire of a woman, grabbed God by the collar and told him how this was all going to go down. At least that's how I imagined it between him and her.

For a while, Eric and I were just glad to have found a home that fit our family—a great neighborhood with kind folks, a school at the end of our street, a cobblestone patio where we'd linger for most of our summers. But it didn't take long to feel the walls of our already small home constricting and contracting; the foundation squeezing in with each inch our kids grew, with each friend we added to our lives, with each moment worth celebrating for which we didn't have the space. The life I'd always dreamed I'd have within the walls of my home was gradually compressing into a vapor of misty smoke.

My longing for the house I desire is frequent, persistent, and intense. I long for a gathering place where friends amply commune around my table, casually passing plates while comfortable in their own skin; a safe haven for my children to invite their friends to, a simple space to hang out as the people they'll someday become; a respite where extended family comes to visit for Thanksgiving as I fling open the doors because I have plenty of room to house them, feed them, and watch them nap after dinner; a hub of celebration when life's most precious moments are too important to let them blur by in a tornado of hasty debris. Some will argue that hospitality is a way of life, an attitude of the heart, and I do understand that to be true, but I also live with the reality that the hospitable life I desire is dampened by the physical limitations of the space in which I live. And so instead of flinging wide our doors, we let others entertain us—again and again and again—always happy to bring the casserole but knowing we will rarely be able to return the favor, knowing we have little hope for anything different. And this is always the hardest part.

And so with each weary breath, I muster the energy to tell myself again: *Suanne, it's just a house.*

Then why does it feel like so much more?

Perhaps because it's in the physical trappings of this world that we're reminded of that which we most desire that we do not possess, of the crumbs that pass through our fingers that, desperate to hold on to, we watch helplessly as they fall to the floor.

We long for relationships we've never had, intimacy we've never known, joy, peace, contentment that escapes with the fickleness of a hopping toad. We long for wounds to stop bleeding, forgiveness to begin healing, and disease to relent. We long to create, to work, to matter, to love, to know and be known. We long for purpose, for our toil to explode with meaning when it lands on the shoulders of another life. We long to be remembered in a world filled with noise, to live in such a way that when memories illumine and fade in the hearts of others, they are savored with fondness, even if it's only by those few souls who had the courage to dance alongside us through the muck and mundane. And of course there's the most difficult longing of all, the kind that comes with death, the longing that leaves us looking to the clouds and wondering when perfection will descend from heaven once again.

This is the way it is with life, and this is the way it is with the Stirring. We often have no choice but to live with the longing in both the doing and the becoming, to accept the difficult truth that maybe we're not living the life we've always imagined ourselves living or that we will never achieve all that we've aspired to accomplish or that there will always be a version of ourselves that we long to become that will, despite each good intention, be smothered by the dirt of our sin.

We are a people who long.

Perhaps the most delicate (and maddening) intricacy of longing, and what sets it apart from our dreams, is that, by definition, it is a persistent desire for unattainable things. Dreams, on the contrary, no matter how distant, hold within them embers of starry inspiration that leave us tingling with hope; dreams put a finger under our chins and gently lift our eyes toward the blue ocean of possibility, the glow of the sun-kissed sky. (Even broken dreams can have elements of realization along the way, even if they are ultimately lost.) Longing, on the other hand, propels us into the dark holes of our souls, shining light on those things that we yearn for so deeply but have little hope of ever coming to be. *Saudade* the Portuguese call it. "A vague and constant desire," says Portuguese scholar Aubrey Bell in his 1912 book *In Portugal*, "for something that does not and probably cannot exist, for something other than the present." As we grapple with our longings, we face the stark reality that they very well may spend a lifetime lying with the crumbs on the floor.

In case I haven't been clear: I am a person who longs.

Longing is anguish. And yet longing is beauty. Its paradox carries within it a mixture of pain and grace that causes the human race to thirst for that which is unquenchable, but also that which will someday drift from outside the reach of our fingers and slide to rest in the palms of our hands. Because the truth about longing is this: it rightfully reminds us that God pressed eternity into the fabric of humanity so that when yearning moans from the deepest recesses of who we are, we have no choice but to wet our lips with the sound of his name and beg for the only home that will ever satisfy all of our needs. The unattainable nature of *suadade* postures us toward paradise like nothing else can.

And so longing must be confessed. And longing must be embraced. And longing, if it is not to suffocate us as we wrestle with the Stirring, must always be accompanied by faith, faith that there is a vast space that one day will relieve us from the aches of this earth, like a chronic illness at last exonerating us from its relentless grip, and the peace of heaven will absolve us from all that is not yet. The unattainable will finally be made whole. For longing without faith is longing without hope—and that's not the people we've become.

I eventually get myself out the door. After three years of commuting to the city, I've become accustomed to the routine, and yet the commute seems to get longer with each passing day. The Stirring presses in, and I wonder if my job at the nonprofit is a good fit for who I've become during these last ten years. I wonder if it's time for a change. I wonder what it'd be like to risk life in an entirely new direction. Longing seeps for something that holds the vagueness of *suadade*, and I immediately chastise myself for how quickly discontentment creeps when life is actually pretty good.

I'm reminded of a story Carla told me about her dad, who passed away last year at the age of ninety-four, peaceful in his sleep with his son-in-law at his side. During the months leading up to his death, Carla told me repeatedly that he was ready to die, ready to let go of this life and finally see what the fuss of heaven was all about. During those same months, his health in decline, Carla wrestled with the idea of bringing him back to Chicago to live with her. When she mentioned the idea to his doctor, an eighty-one-year-old gem who still made house calls, he cautioned her against removing him from his home. Then he told Carla something she shared over breakfast one morning that immediately struck a chord: "There are three things every soul needs to survive," he said, "to be known, to have purpose, and to be remembered." Removing someone from their home, he said, can threaten all three.

I turn it over in my mind, let it soak with the truth of my longing. Our dreams and our longings often become so entangled we lose sight of how to pull them apart, to separate their strings and put each in its rightful place. A space exists between them in which we need to make peace. We need to make peace with our home.

The first signs of spring are budding with patches of bright yellow greens. I've traded my down parka for a light wool coat, snow boots for brown rubber Hunters. The sun is radiant, and as the city comes into view, a light glow (or perhaps a misty haze) hangs over the outline of the skyscrapers. I decide it's pretty, despite its hostile encumbrance of cement and metal.

The train shifts hard to the left, then knocks back to the right, and I immediately make a decision: I'm not going to let the bouncing, no matter how jarring, take the peace of this moment away.

19

Faithfulness

*Perseverance is not the result of our determination, it is the result
of God's faithfulness. . . . Perseverance is triumphant and alive.*

EUGENE PETERSON,
A LONG OBEDIENCE IN THE SAME DIRECTION

How long do I need to sit here?
It's often the first thought I think when I sit down to write.
How long do I need to sit here until I can feel like I accomplished enough that I can finally walk away?

A friend of mine once told me to write toward truth.

A noble idea.

I thought I would try it for a while.

And so I have a ritual when I write.

I take *The Sacred Journey* by Frederick Buechner out of my backpack and set it on the table next to me, always on the right. Today I take it out of a cracked and worn, stepped-on, spilled-on Whole Foods bag and set it directly next to my coffee, the one with the steamed cream and two raw sugars. The cover is worn, the edges frayed, and the entire book has a hard warped-ness to it from the time I left it in between the seats of my minivan and Sadie's water bottle saturated its pages. I had to use a hairdryer to salvage the pages, something I've never told my friend Jeff, who sacrificially gave me his own autographed copy as a parting gift from our time together as coworkers, his kind way of inspiring me to step into my own dream to create—and the reason I've never tried to give it back.

After the spill, I spent the first year or more berating myself for the accident, the way my carelessness caused the red ink of a Pulitzer Prize–nominated autograph to fade to blush and dribble down the page. But during that same year, grace had been doing a work in my heart, the way only grace can, and so I slowly learned to appreciate the character the imperfection adds, the way the dribble gives something that was already cherished its own unique story. No other copy of this book looks like mine; no other copy holds this particular story.

Sometimes, I pick the book up and let it linger in my hands, feeling the gravitas of the way words can change the world and the souls of those who inhabit it. I flip through a few pages and skim a story here and there, pausing now and then to jot down a quote or underline brilliant prose, but mostly I simply let the words pour over me, seep into my pores, trickle into my soul, water slipping through rocks in a slow-moving creek, until that thing that's deep inside, the place where inspiration and belief and passion collide, begins to stir and bubble on its own accord.

Other times I don't.

Other times I just let it lie there, allowing the picture on the front cover to have its way with me, the picture of Frederick's dad holding him as a baby, his father's strong arm wrapped around his midsection, his colossal hand covering his son's small torso. I wonder how many years after his father's suicide Frederick pulled this picture out; I wonder if it was a keepsake he had tucked away in his nightstand or if he happened upon it unexpectedly, years after the fact, in a way that stole his breath, transporting him back to that one awful morning when his life changed forever. I wonder how this picture stirs his own soul.

Whatever I choose to do with it at any given time, the book has become a reminder of a friend's command as he spoke into my vocational life: whatever you write, be sure to write toward truth. In other words, dig deeper than you thought you could. Reach inside and bring to light that which causes you to live more honestly than you ever thought you could.

Not a bad way to live.

On this particular Sunday morning, however, I look at the picture of Frederick and find my resolve waning. I'm sitting in a folding plastic chair at a folding plastic table at Sadie's youth volleyball tournament. This is often how I've found myself writing. The warehouse-type gym is filled, if I had to guess, with nearly six hundred people. There are twelve courts, games happening on each; the sharp sounds of whistles darting, yellow jackets skimming my head. Swells of cheers crescendo and decelerate; coaches yell at referees; parents yell at kids. A two-room inflatable bounce house contains the screams of a dozen toddlers behind me. This is not uncommon of the space I find myself in as I try to write toward truth, and probably how most of us try to live toward the Stirring. Sitting in my car as I wait for practice to end, swaying on the train as I make my way to work, blocking out the noise of the bleachers as I wait for the game to start, drowning out the voices in a congested coffee shop. This is the life I have in which to try to carve out a dent in the world. A team of girls in blue uniforms with matching ribbons and braids converges on the table next to me, less than a foot away, and busts out their loudest rendition of Miley

Cyrus's "Hoedown Throwdown," pounding the table in cascading rhythms. My soul moans.

I scan the gym, which is roughly the size of a couple of airplane hangars, and cynically wonder if any other moms or parents or bystanders are here watching their daughters play volleyball while they're trying to live toward truth in the midst of all the noise.

I look at my word count and see that I've only typed 165 words. And I find myself thinking it again: *how long do I need to sit here?*

Tchaikovsky's 1812 Overture is fifteen minutes long. Most people will only recognize the last two minutes of it, the part with the cannons and the fireworks.

I came to this realization as I sat listening to the Boston Pops perform the piece on the lawn of their famous outdoor amphitheater, Tanglewood. Named after a book by Nathaniel Hawthorne, Tanglewood is a breathtaking 210-acre landscape of sprawling lawns, paved walkways, 10-foot royal hedges, and perfectly manicured grounds. I sat in a lawn chair next to Eric, my uncle, and a bottle of red wine, my kids sprawled on a blanket at our feet. The Overture was the climax of the evening, the piece de resistance of the night. After two hours of sleepy compositions that none of us recognized, I nudged Sadie and Clay awake with my foot. They groaned.

As the Overture finally began, a childlike anticipation welled inside me. Not because I was a classical music fan (not by any stretch of the imagination), but because I was just culturally refined enough to know that Tchaikovsky's 1812 Overture performed live by the Boston Pops at Tanglewood was a pretty big deal.

I waited for greatness.

It took me about ten seconds to realize that I didn't recognize the song. Not hardly at all.

As the beginning rolled along, I strained to hear even a hint of the familiar. I had the fleeting thought of mouthing some ignorant words to my New England uncle, "*Are you sure this is it?*" Instead, I did what most of us do for a good portion of our lives: I faked it, nodding my head in appreciation, pretending it was as recognizable to me as it was to the pretentious middle-aged couple sitting next to us who had, two hours earlier, shushed my kids for crunching their crackers too loudly.

It didn't take long, however, to forget what I did or didn't recognize and to get lost in the magic of the evening—the beauty of the music, the austerity of the space we were in, the awe of the giftedness that poured from the stage, the feel of the August humidity damp on my skin. I laid my head back, closed my eyes, and breathed it in, once even lifting my hands, just a few inches above my chair, palms up, letting the exquisiteness of it all run through my fingers. It felt like church on a Sunday morning.

And I waited for the cannons.

Later, I thought about how difficult it must have been for Tchaikovsky to write that piece (how difficult it must be for any musician to write any piece), how many hours he must have labored to get it just right. I imagined crumpled pieces of paper strewn across the floor, eraser marks left above notes no violinist or flautist would ever play. I imagined all the hours no one ever saw, all the mistakes no one would ever hear. And I marveled over how every step he took—misguided, disastrous, joyful, painful—eventually got him to where he wanted to go.

Probably because he never lost sight of where he was headed.

A few months after the Overture, I stood in my brother Jamie's three-car garage. He lives where I've always dreamed of living, on the Farm, across the shallow hollow where, if you look through the trees in the late fall or early spring, you can see my parents' house.

Years ago, before he had a wife and three kids, before he had a girlfriend or any money, he dreamed of building a house and raising kids on the Farm, the same land where he grew up building forts and riding bikes and where we'd played football in the yard, where he killed his first buck and went sledding down hills that were lined with ditches and briar patches that were too steep for him and his friends to be plummeting down. More than any of the rest of us, the Farm has made him who he is.

He spent years of his young adult life going into the woods, pulling out logs that had fallen from old cherry trees, some that had been cut and left for dead by lumberjacks who'd carefully surveyed the land. He'd drag them up and over the steep hills, sometimes hundreds of feet ("you should see some of the hills I dragged them up," he said), to what we fondly called the Old Garage where they'd age and dry for the next fifteen years. He thought maybe someday he'd use them for something, maybe to build his house. On this sticky September day, as I stood in the garage of his new house—the one that sat on the exact spot he proposed to his wife and two years later where we'd gathered in the barren field and listened as Eric married them with vows from the book of Ruth and on which we were standing now—he showed me, a jigsaw and sander between us, how he'd planed the wood, sanded it, cut it, stained it, and how he'd worked most evenings and weekends in that garage for more than a year to make it the trim in his house, the house he now shares with his wife and kids he didn't then know he'd ever had.

The weight of the moment hung so beautifully I thought I might cry.

The music of the Overture began to build, the now familiar cadence speeding up. I sat up straighter. I tapped my foot. Sadie and Clay jolted awake. The anticipation was electric. When the cannons came, they didn't disappoint. We could feel the boom vibrate through our heels, electric shocks sent to the core of the earth. The climax wasn't overrated, just like the Eiffel Tower hadn't been overrated when I'd first seen it in Paris or how the view of the Chicago skyline from a Lake Michigan sailboat never ceases to leave me breathless. It was as magnificent and soul filling and heart thumping as it promised to be. More cannons exploded. Flashes of white brilliance abounded. Cheers erupted. Any question in my mind about dragging Eric and the kids to this place dissipated in the twinkling of the stars. It was nothing less than magical.

On the drive back to the house, as the swell started to fade, I began to think about the other thirteen minutes of the Overture, the ones I didn't recognize, the ones before the cannons. They were just as beautiful, but most probably wouldn't recognize or care about them, just like most of us wouldn't recognize the sounds of our lives if we didn't take the time to stop and listen.

This is how dreams find their beginning, one inaugural sound whose vibrations we must faithfully follow regardless if anyone recognizes their music, every note a poignant and necessary guidepost along the way. "What a long time," says Parker Palmer, "it's taken to be the person we've always wished to become."

For all of my talk of pressing on and believing, there is one truth I've perhaps alluded to but sadly failed to exhume this far: through all of our searching and prodding and intentionality and becoming, we need to quickly understand that living toward truth is not about our faithfulness to God but about his faithfulness to us. "Perseverance is not the result of our determination," Eugene Peterson said, it is the result of God's faithfulness. We survive in the way of faith not because we have extraordinary stamina but because God is righteous, because God sticks with us, . . . finding the meaning of our lives not by probing our moods and motives and morals but by believing in God's will and purposes; making a map of the faithfulness of God, not charting the rise and fall of our enthusiasms. It is out of such a reality that we acquire perseverance. Perseverance is triumphant and alive.

Perseverance is like the thirteen minutes.

We're so tempted to just see the ending. We hear the cannons and the climax and our insides swell up and we get a pounding in our chest and we want all of life to be this way. We want all of it to be about the cannons and the crashing and the stunning white flashes and the way it all makes us feel, swept up in the beauty and majesty and wonder of life. And that's okay because those moments are sweet and beautiful and are what keep us going through the mundane and the mire and the hard and the boring—those flashes of greatness and glory and beauty that we know exist, in the presence and talents of others, in the outer edges of the world, looming, waiting for someone to see and experience in all of their imperial majesty.

And sometimes they lie right inside of us.

God never gives up on his pursuit of wooing us to become, to know and to make known, to explore the things he's been whispering so sweetly and intimately, pushing us and challenging us to offer ourselves to the sounds of our lives and to the Stirring, because he never gives up on us. It doesn't matter if our dreams, i.e., what we do, ever actually come to fruition. He loves and pursues us in the long redeeming love story, and he'll continue to pursue us until eternity rescues us, transforming our sorrows and failures and sin and shame. He'll find us in the depths of the basement in a small-town church and within the skyscrapers of the world's biggest cities; he'll find us at our kitchen tables and our bathroom floors. And both in the end and along the way, he won't care what we accomplish but how much we became more like him. He won't care, as Madeline L'Engle says, about how much we know, but about how much he knows us. We'll walk in the paradox of the dust and the world and the beauty and the ashes and the reality of all of its messed up brokenness—and we'll put one foot in front of the other and do the best we can, by his grace, until we can't do it anymore.

And we'll let go, once again, of all that we want to do and ask who we want to be.

For it is not we who are faithful to God, but God who is faithful to us.

> But it was because the LORD loved you and kept the oath he swore to your ancestors that he brought you out with a mighty hand and redeemed you from the land of slavery, from the power of Pharaoh king of Egypt. Know therefore that the LORD your God is God; he is the faithful God, keeping his covenant of love to a thousand generations of those who love him and keep his commandments. (Deuteronomy 7:8-9)

When the orchestra sits silent and the anticipation of the first sound reverberates through the audience; when the conductor raises his hand, when the instruments are raised to position; when he points to his left and the percussionist strikes just one key, we know without a doubt that it is the first sound. The first sound of many to come that lead us to our own climax, one that's roaring with cannons or fireworks or one that's completely void of them, whatever that may be. It doesn't matter because God is working in front of us and behind us and on each side of us, all the while or- chestrating our lives from their conception as he works out his divine purposes in his kingdom, both within us and among us, both now and yet to come.

His is the first drop, the first ping, the first sound that echoes throughout the audience.

His is the first sound of a million dreams.

A million dreams that sway, wheat dancing in the wind, pulling and prodding us to become.

A million dreams made of a million sounds that make us who we are.

And so we sit there as long as it takes.

20

Beautiful

It takes courage to grow up and become who you really are.

E. E. CUMMINGS

I was once part of a discussion in which a group of friends were trying to define beauty. None of the answers, including my own, were alluring until my friend Sarah said *I think God is beautiful*. After this dream, I know she is right.

I am in a house I don't recognize, a house with a maze of unending rooms, every door leading to another room with another door. I open and close for a long time until the last door leads to a set of rickety stairs, at the top of which is a walk-in attic with cobwebs and boxes and faint rays of sunlight poking through cracks in the ceiling. It reminds me of a movie scene where the granddaughter blows the dust off some trinket she finds in the bottom of some box, a family heirloom that reveals the secrets of a sordid family history: the brother she never knew she had, the unabated love her mother had for another man, the unlawful mystery that had never been unearthed. I linger in this room for only a few moments before I'm transported into a small courtyard shared by four 1950s-style apricot brick homes.

In the middle of the courtyard, surrounded by bright colored petunias, is a statue of Jesus. It's made of the kind of gray stone you'd pass on the front lawn of a garden shop next to a frog wearing a tuxedo or a cherub with hair curling wildly around its ears. A small fountain trickles next to it. I look up at the house and recognition slowly dawns; I'm standing outside of my sister-in-law's house, a house owned by her grandmother, passed down to her dad and where she now lives with my brother. I feel drawn to the statue in a way I can't explain, sirens singing from the rocks, and so I reach out my hand to touch it. Only before I can touch it, the praying hands of Jesus come out of position and he touches me, his hand encircling my forearm.

Transcendent.

The sensation I don't have words to describe. Nothing quite fits. I could say it was warm, two steps warmer than luke but not yet hot, and that it started where he touched my forearm and it spread, seeping through my body until every blood vessel was full and flowing, every nerve ending stretching, reaching as far as it could until it burst from my fingertips, electric, a witch casting a spell, but it fails to capture the earnestness of it. I could say it was peaceful, like watching a great blue heron soar from the sway of a mountain dock while the glow of the sun dipped below the horizon, but it fails to capture the gloriousness of it. I could say it was loving, like the way a heart feels when the breath of a child's innocence wets the nape of its neck, but it fails to capture the tenderness of it. It was all of those things, but none of those things. It was so much more. It was, I think, what heaven must feel like. What God must feel like. Not what he feels like, but what he is. He is beautiful. And he touched me.

Exquisite.

His touch woke me from my dream, transcending the chasm between wake and sleep, fantasy and reality, within its grasp lying a palpitation of no tears, no sorrow, no death, no pain, no mourning; the carcass of the old tumbling and fading until only grace was left. Grace at its quintessential best, an unnecessary reminder from the throne of heaven itself, one that didn't wait for me to reach up to it, but one that spanned the expanse of time and reached me first—because that's the only way he knows how to exist. I woke not with a memory but a feeling as real as anything I'd ever experienced. Peace I had never known. Convinced as I'd ever been that God exists, that he is real, that he is love, and that he touched me—for almost no reason at all.

Because that, in his kindness, is simply what God does. Because that's simply who he is.

Not all dreams happen while we sleep.

While the sleeping dreams hold the power to whisper to us from the mysteries that lie deep beneath the threshold of consciousness within both the physical and the spiritual realms, reminding us that every wink of creation is prodigiously at work as we listen to the Stirring, calling us to risk the giving of our everyday lives to sounds that are greater than ourselves—they are fleeting. They leave an impression, a memory imbedded with significant meaning and emotion, but in the end, most are a vision that will never exist.

Other dreams we carry while we're awake. They swim through our mind, pound in our chest, vibrate in our heart, keep us up at night. They fuel us. They are visions of all we're meant to do and all we're meant to become. They are the dreams where God transcends and touches us. They are beauty and grace. They hold the power to change the whole world or just our small corners of it. They are fuzzy; dreams whose center may be clear but whose edges are frayed. We scrunch up our foreheads, we squint, we try so hard to see them, yet like the vanishing details of a fantasy from which we wake, or a memory we can't make resurface, we simply can't see them.

But the Stirring in our soul remains.

And so we get up each day and we put one foot in front of the other. Unsure and insecure, hurried and afraid, tired and overwhelmed, we, by faith, pick up the things that are placed in front of us. We work tirelessly at the dreams that stir inside of us for an outcome we're not sure will ever come to pass.

And just when we think we've made the whole thing up, just when we think the finitude of the ashes will overtake us, we remember that Jesus touched us. That the feeling was real because in all of our searching, there are no words to describe his embrace; nothing on earth can compare. And when we close our eyes and imagine it, we can feel it all over again. And then we know that it's real, and that we can trust, and that we can have confidence in what we hope for and assurance about that which we do not see.

Because we actually felt the touch of God.

And it was beautiful.

And so we carry on with our dreams for just one more day.

You are but dust. The world was created for you.

And in the midst of carrying on, we loosen our grip on the dreams and the Stirring, opening our hands to let their threads spill outside our own ashen frame. We marvel over the web that clings so delicately between our own desire and the hands of a humble King. We rest. We trust—peaceful, satisfied—as the sounds of holiness envelope us. We offer ourselves to our dreams a million times—again and again and again—and with each offering, we become more content to simply sit at the mercy of his love and grace. That is, to simply become.

Epilogue

In My Wildest Dreams

*The world is wilder than that in all
directions, more dangerous and bitter, more
extravagant and bright. We are making hay when
we should be making whoopee; we are raising tomatoes
when we should be raising Cain, or Lazarus.*

ANNIE DILLIARD, *PILGRIM AT TINKER CREEK*

Not in my wildest dreams.
People say this and it makes me sad. If your dreams can't come true in your wildest dreams, then what hope do they possibly have?

I got carry-out and sat in my hotel room. Alone and claustro-phobic in the confines of its scratchy quilts and wall-to-wall drap-eries. Alone on this Friday night. Alone in the world.

I was at a conference, one that I contentedly, even ardently, went to—alone. Between commuting and working and wifing and mothering, I hadn't had much space to nurture my creative soul.

This was a respite and it was good. On the three-hour drive there, I couldn't help but reflect on the contrast of my previous visits to this place. I'd been here twice before, the first as a hopeful romantic on a weekend soiree; the second as part of my job that I didn't yet have the first time I went. The first time I'd been here, about four years before, I sat in a hearty Irish pub with my manuscript group as we'd hoisted aspirations filled with golden pints of beer, a toast to the new group we'd officially named in honor of the budding Michigan trees.

To say the group was life giving at the early point of the Stirring would be an understatement. It was the first community I'd ever been part of that intuitively understood the Stirring, because in their own way, they'd all felt it too. Month after month we gathered; they encouraged me to find my voice, and in turn, I think I helped them find theirs too. Like any group with a common affinity, we commiserated over the frustrations we uniquely shared, celebrated one another's successes, and rallied together over the collective belief that we really could change the whole world. In the process, we became more than respected colleagues and budding artists; we became friends. Over the next couple of years, I watched as each woman, one by one, published their first books (and then sometimes their second) all the while silently pleading that God might kindly grant my turn.

By the second time I went to the conference, our small manuscript group had grown into a national writer's collective. The realization of the impact didn't dawn until we hosted our own reception at the conference, hoping a handful of people would come to save us the embarrassment of a complete flop of a night. To our astonishment, the room we rented quickly became packed with industry professionals—authors, editors, agents—who graced us with their presence. I stood in the midst of the clinking and mingling and chatter, steeped in conversation with another member, unaware of the totality of the crowd until we finally picked up our heads for the first time and allowed our eyes to drink in the room. The substance of what we'd accomplished gradually settled in. We'd actually pulled this thing off.

In our wildest dreams.

Six months before the third time I attended the conference, our group fell apart. The details of the events precipitating the unraveling are not mine to share, but they resulted in ten of my thirteen pint-raising friends resigning their post in less than a week. My decision to not be among them resulted in one of the more difficult paths I've traveled. Not only was I grieving the loss of the community I had so intensely come to love, I was trying to navigate the aftermath of waters that were more complex than I had the intellectual skill or emotional capacity to bear. I carried the anxiety like a sandbag on my chest for the next five months before resigning myself. It was also why, my third time at this conference, I sat in a hotel room alone, feeling the depths of loneliness in a way I hadn't felt since we first moved to Chicago, over a cold plate of pasta and a bottle of red wine—the sacrifice of choosing the narrow road stinging with full force.

The next morning I crammed the remnants of my self-pity into a pair of cute boots and made my way to a luncheon. I'd been invited to celebrate a line of books I had helped to create during my time at the publishing house. It was my last official act before I made the drive home and one I barely mustered the emotional energy for, but I was excited to see my old colleagues and curious to see what the lunch was all about. (Weeks before, when I wondered why they invited me aloud, aspiration dripping tentatively from my voice, Eric quipped, "They were probably just being nice." I found myself immediately assuming he was right.) I sat at the u-shaped table across from many of the women I used to know so well, again feeling the shrinking inadequacy of being the only one who hadn't accomplished my dreams. A part of me couldn't wait to escape, to climb into the safety of my car and let the floodgates crash.

The luncheon came to a close, and I thanked the editor for the invitation, still a little perplexed about how I'd made the list. After a few pleasantries, she dropped her voice and whispered out of the corner of her mouth, "There are a lot of people who'd love to see you write. I'd be happy to take a look."

In my wildest dreams.

I twisted my hands in a myriad of shapes. My mind flashed back to the conversation I had with my editor friend in his office now six years before, the one where I told him I thought I'd like to write about dreams. I thought back to all the exasperating conversations Eric had endured when I first thought I wanted to write.

"So what is it you want to write about?" he'd ask.

"I'm not sure," I'd say, staring vacantly at the trickling stone waterfall, peace, in our backyard.

Silence.

"Well, what do you want people to do when they finish reading it?"

"I don't know," I said. "Learn something I guess. Something about themselves, something about God. I want them to reflect on their life."

"Oh, then you can have steps at the end of each chapter. Things they can do?"

"Well, um, maybe. But I don't think so."

More silence.

I thought about all the hours I'd spent sitting at coffee shops writing about nothing, everything, all the dinners that went unmade and bathrooms unkempt. I thought about all the angst the Stirring had caused, all the doubt and insecurity and depression and fist-pounding rants. And I thought about the way grace had overtaken me in each and every one.

I thought about the postcard my friend Tracey gave me years ago, the one that still hangs on my refrigerator underneath the picture of Sadie's fourth birthday party, the one we had right before we moved to Chicago.

Line one: *That's a crazy idea. Insane. It doesn't make sense.*

Line two: You'll do it, then?

Line three: *Of course, I replied.*

On the back she'd written, "Sweet friend, saw this and thought of you. I am forever and always cheering you on to every good thing God leads you to."

My mind jolted back to the present.

"I've been working on something for a while," I said. "I might be close."

I was mostly bluffing. I'd been working on something for a long while, like the last eight years, but I didn't feel even remotely close.

As I drove home that day, I thought of the first time I felt the Stirring, the voices who'd named me along the way; I thought of the risks I'd taken, the hours spent during early mornings and late nights scouring for ideas, feeding my creative soul, scurrying for deadlines; I thought of the humiliating failures, the loss of relationships, my shame and disappointment and all the ways I failed at the becoming. I thought of my childhood dreams. I thought of how Eric and I kicked up our feet, staring at that twenty-five-dollar Walmart Christmas tree with no idea how life would unfold.

And I thought of how kind Jesus was, how kind he always is, and how his grace is big enough for all of it, in the face of a million things.

And then I remembered once again the words of Kathleen Norris.

"I can't imagine why God would want me, of all people, as an offering. But if God is foolish enough to take me as I am, I guess I'd better do it."

And so I offered myself once again.

Acknowledgments

A friend of mine once said that there are two things most likely to change a person: the books they read and the people they meet. I have been profoundly shaped by both. I am forever indebted to the excellence of writers like Frederick Buechner, Parker Palmer, Anne Lamott, Donald Miller, and Barbara Brown Taylor, whose words have inspired me—both by the depth of their meaning and by the beauty in which they were woven together. I have spent hours poring over their work, stunned. I wouldn't have labored without their investment in the craft, and for that I am grateful.

Thank you to the team of folks at InterVarsity Press who have taken such good care of me, chief among them my editor, Cindy Bunch, who has been gentle, patient, and insightful as I've labored through my first book. Thank you also to the entire editorial, marketing, and production teams without whose hard work no book would ever come to life, including the amazing cover design of Cindy Kiple, an unsung hero.

Thank you to Christen Schmeltz, Jeff Crosby, and Melissa Sandy for reading the first draft of this work and giving me your thoughtful feedback. This book wouldn't be the same without you; I hope you see your fingerprints trickled through each page. Thank you to Roger and Carla Peer, Ben and Nancy Cremer, and Duane and Jeannine Steiner for giving me the gift of space by opening your homes while you were away. Thank you to Dave and Beth Booram for following your own dreams to Sustainable Faith Indy and providing the most holy writing experience I've ever known. This book wouldn't be possible without any of you.

For as long as I've carried the dream to write a book, countless people have carried this dream with me, believing in me, encouraging me—and listening to me agonize every step of the way, all in varying degrees. I will never be able to name each one here, but several have deposited belief in me at exactly the right time; I am convinced I wouldn't have had the courage to write without your collective voice: Dan Meyer, Lisa Garvin, Ruthanne Focht, Mark and Randi Lundgren, Amy Schubert, Betty Brandolino, Kathy Ashcroft, Dave Zimmerman, Jerry Sloan, Pete Creamer, Ed Uszynski, Wade and Tonia Hardtke, Angie Weszely, Anita Lustrea, Elisa Morgan, and Jen Pollock Michel. Thank you also to the wonderful family of Christ Church of Oak Brook for allowing me to find my voice in your midst, graciously watching me stumble along (and picking me up) in front of your very eyes, and to the founders of the Redbud Writers Guild for inspiring me to find my voice in the first place. Thank you (more than words!) to my sisters at Caris and Luminate Marketing for your laughter, friendship, consummate encouragement, and perpetual embodiment of grace.

There are two people who, without, this book never would have come to be. Thank you to Adele Calhoun for believing in me at the onset of the Stirring and for being the first person to ask who I wanted to be. Thank you to Jeff Crosby for introducing me to great writing, for your friendship, and for your influence in so many areas of my becoming; you are most often the one person who believes in me more than I believe in myself.

I'd be nowhere without friends who nurture my spirit far beyond my writing life. Thank you to Amy Uszynski and Sarah Keefer for being two of the most beautiful souls I know and for making me closer to Jesus just by calling you friends. Thank you to Rebecca Wells and Nicole Truax for being my first friends in Chicago, for allowing me the joy of your families, and for always accepting me exactly as I am. Thank you to Carla Peer for three years of the best breakfasts I've ever known, for always pushing me to listen to God, to lift my eyes out of the busyness of life and to see matters of eternity, and for your prayers. And thank you to Nancy Cremer, Amy McCurry, and Tracey Bianchi for walking through every inch of life with me regardless of where it's taken us, knowing me more intimately than any friends I've ever had—and choosing to love me anyway. I couldn't breathe without any of you.

I wouldn't be who I am without the influence of two amazing families. Thank you to the Camfield family for welcoming me as your own, and to the entire Ashcroft family who has shaped me more than any words will ever describe. To my sisters-in-law, Sharon, Amber, and Jen, for always inquiring about this project and cheering me on. To my cousin Mindy, who shines light into my deepest insecurities and makes me feel like I can change the world, and who makes me laugh harder than anyone I know with the wit of her words. To my brothers, Jamie and David, for sharing your lives with me from my very first days and being constant companions of love and support—and for the hours of memories on the Farm that I've savored with joy as I've written each word of this book. To my sister Bobbi, my best friend for thirty-plus years, for being the first person I ever wanted to be like. Your unending supply of grace, encouragement, and unconditional friendship sustain me. You are the one person I could not survive life without. And to my parents, Rich and Barb Ashcroft, whose investment in lives stretches near and far, but none more deeply than within our own family. Thank you for allowing me the privilege of watching you live out the values that have most shaped who I am, and for your constant love.

I never dreamed I could love two people as much as I love the ones who God is daily shaping before my very eyes. To my daughter, Sadie, for being a woman of strength, courage, and boldness, who inspires me to give all I have to whatever I do and to dream bigger dreams. And to my son, Clay, for being a young man of creativity, character, and kindness. Your thoughtfulness fills my heart until it's overflowing; you remind me to pursue the tenderness of God. Being your mom has been the greatest joy of my life.

Lastly, to Eric. To say you are my partner or my best friend doesn't do our marriage justice. Thank you for sacrificing in so many areas of your life to make this book possible, for weathering the emotional ups and downs with a steady and encouraging spirit, for always challenging me to live from a deeper place, and for teaching me more about Jesus than any person I know. Your gifts have enabled me to follow the sound of my dreams, and for that, I am eternally grateful.

All glory to God the Father, the Son, and the Holy Spirit. For everything comes from him and exists by his power and is intended for his glory. All glory to him forever. Amen. (Romans 11:36)